SIMPLY DEMI-VEG

SIMPLY DEMI-VEG

David Scott

Thorsons
An Imprint of HarperCollins*Publishers*

Thorsons
An Imprint of HarperCollins*Publishers*
77–85 Fulham Palace Road,
Hammersmith, London W6 8JB

Published by Thorsons 1993
10   9   8   7   6   5   4   3   2   1

A catalogue record for this book
is available from the British Library

ISBN 0 7225 2765 9

Illustration on p.2 by Jenny Dooge

Typeset by Harper Phototypesetters Limited,
Northampton, England
Printed in Great Britain by
HarperCollinsManufacturing Glasgow

CONTENTS

ACKNOWLEDGEMENTS

I would like to thank Eve Bletcher, home economist and food stylist, and Diny Zalk, a talented amateur cook, for their immense help in the preparation of this book. Many thanks also to Rita Trotter for her continued expert typing and layout of my book manuscripts.

INTRODUCTION

A few years ago I was mulling over similarities I had noticed between the country cooking of Japan (a special interest of mine), the dietary habits of other established peasant cultures, and recent changes in customers' eating patterns at the restaurant in which I am a partner. The phrase that came to my lips to describe the link between them was 'demi-vegetarian diet'. This summed up in a simple way the diets of these disparate groups of people, and it also found a resonance with friends I tested it on. It's not a very elegant phrase but people immediately recognized its meaning and said, 'Oh yes, I'm a demi-vegetarian, have been for ages.' As it turned out, the phrase was not original after all, and as I signed a contract to write a book on the same theme (*The Demiveg Cookbook*), the Fresh Fruit and Vegetable Board were launching a new 'Demiveg' promotion. We had both alighted on the same phrase to describe a way of eating that was and is rapidly growing in popularity.

The definitions of what constitutes a demi-vegetarian are probably as numerous as the people who describe themselves as such, but for me the ideal demi-vegetarian diet gives gastronomic pleasure and promotes optimum health. It is composed of plant foods, with special emphasis on grains (as in bread, pasta, rice, etc.) and fresh fruit and vegetables, plus smaller amounts of fish, chicken and dairy produce. For health or humane reasons red meat is not, or rarely, included in the diet. The ingredients used should be grown or reared in as natural an environment as possible – one that avoids the use of hormones, pesticides, and artificial additives – and as food buyers we should encourage our suppliers to support these aims. Notwithstanding this, I would not recommend food faddism, and if you wish to eat refined foods such as rich cream cakes now and again, then enjoy yourself and do not feel guilty about it. As someone once said, 'Guilt is a four-letter word!'

The term demi-vegetarian is new, but the concept is not. If one looks at what is traditionally judged to be a desirable and healthy way of eating in various cultures around the world it is a demi-vegetarian diet that emerges. For instance, a traditional Japanese meal of rice, tofu, pickles and fish; the Mexican peasant meal of refried beans, cornmeal tortillas, cheese or meat, lettuce, tomatoes and onions; or the Middle Eastern street food of pitta bread stuffed with chickpea rissoles, raw vegetables and yogurt. Grains and vegetables are considered primary foods, with fish, poultry, beans, fruit and dairy products (or soya bean products in the East) playing essential supporting roles.

Finally, it is worth adding that whatever name we give it, for me, there is no such thing as the perfect diet. Each of us has unique requirements and even these change depending on our age, state of health, work and numerous other factors. Thus, to evolve a good diet for ourselves we need to develop an awareness of our body's needs. This is a difficult task, and sometimes we'll get it right, other times not and sometimes we won't even want to be bothered. Thus flexibility and moderation are perhaps our best twin approaches to developing a sensible diet.

THE DEMI-VEGETARIAN DIET

The illustration overleaf demonstrates graphically the emphasis on particular foods in the demi-vegetarian diet.

Make foods at the top of the triangle the smallest proportion of your diet and those at the bottom the highest.

Seven Steps to a Healthy Demi-vegetarian Diet

1 Include one of the cereal foods, such as bread, pasta, rice or other grains (or potatoes as an alternative) at most meals. Buy wholegrain products such as brown bread, wholemeal pasta etc. most of the time.

2 Eat lots of fruit and vegetables (including raw vegetables in salads) every day. Five portions a day is the ideal.

3 Eat a wide variety of foods and enjoy them. Take advantage of the huge selection of home-produced and imported vegetables, fruits, grains, pulses, cheeses, fish, herbs, spices and the other flavourings now available in shops and supermarkets.

4 Substitute poultry or fish for red meat. Eat fish or poultry no more than two or three times a week respectively.

5 Use semi-skimmed or skimmed milk and take advantage of low-fat dairy products. Eat butter only moderately. For cooking and dressings use vegetable oils such as olive oil, sunflower oil and corn oil. Remember to limit your consumption of all fats and oils.

6 Reduce your intake of sugar, salt and artificial colourings and flavourings. It is easiest to do this by cutting down on processed foods, biscuits, confectionery and snack foods.

7 In conjunction with the first six dietary steps take moderate exercise regularly.

The illustration below demonstrates graphically the emphasis on particular foods in the demivegetarian diet.

Make foods at the top of the triangle the smallest proportion of your diet and those at the bottom the highest.

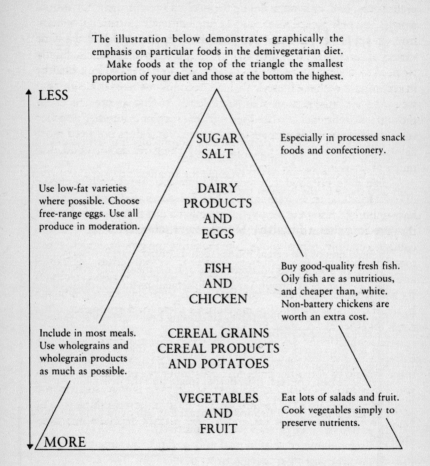

LESS

SUGAR
SALT

Especially in processed snack foods and confectionery.

Use low-fat varieties where possible. Choose free-range eggs. Use all produce in moderation.

DAIRY
PRODUCTS
AND
EGGS

FISH
AND
CHICKEN

Buy good-quality fresh fish. Oily fish are as nutritious, and cheaper than, white. Non-battery chickens are worth an extra cost.

Include in most meals. Use wholegrains and wholegrain products as much as possible.

CEREAL GRAINS
CEREAL PRODUCTS
AND POTATOES

VEGETABLES
AND
FRUIT

Eat lots of salads and fruit. Cook vegetables simply to preserve nutrients.

MORE

Diversity in the Demi-vegetarian Diet

Everyone has unique nutritional needs. We also have individual food preferences, and individual foods themselves vary in their nutritional worth. An apple picked from one tree has a different nutritional content from an apple from another tree. Our needs are thus subject to a wide variety of variables. There are two ways to approach this problem. Firstly we need to develop an awareness of what we need to eat to keep healthy in accordance with the lifestyle we lead. Secondly we need to ensure that we eat a wide cross section of different foods, so that we can cancel out the nutrient deficiencies in one food with the surplus in another, and vice versa. The body needs a range of nutrients, but it does not need more calories than it can burn off. A little of everything can do you good. Too much of anything can be harmful.

A huge variety of food is now available all year round, and the choice of basic foods, such as grains and pulses, increases all the time. We now have unlimited resources for putting together a diet that is enjoyable and that also contributes to our health. The only requirement is that it should contain a combination of foods from the following groups, which, eaten together, fulfil all our nutritional needs: grains and pulses, vegetables and fruit, dairy products, and/or fish and/or poultry. (Vegans can obtain the nutrients found in dairy and fless foods from soya bean products.) In the traditional dishes of many cultures these food groups are often eaten together in the main meal of the day.

Moderation is the key word in changing eating habits. Too much enthusiasm and a crusading zeal usually causes resentment amongst those around us and often precedes backsliding by ourselves. As long as you consistently follow a reasonably good diet there is no reason why you shouldn't treat yourself occasionally. The most important thing is to be happy with the food you eat and to feel neither deprived nor over-indulged.

Fresh, Tinned and Frozen Foods

Fresh foods are high in nutrients and are very important in a demi-vegetarian diet. Whenever possible, buy fresh fruit, vegetables and fish in season. You will then enjoy them at their tastiest and cheapest. Convenience foods can help add variety and speed of preparation to your meals, but avoid any that are highly salted or coloured, have added sugar or are high in fat. Tinned vegetables are fine occasionally if you are in a hurry but the canning process can alter the vitamin content and vegetables are often canned in a very salty solution.

Tinned fruits are sometimes canned in a heavy syrup, so avoid them or use instead fruits that are canned in natural fruit juices. Fresh fruits, like fresh vegetables, generally have a far better flavour and texture than tinned varieties.

Frozen vegetables are quick to prepare and may well be better than poor specimens of the fresh variety. However, sometimes they lose their flavour and texture during freezing or defrosting, and they are usually more expensive than fresh items.

Meal Planning and Entertaining

To plan a meal, choose one or two dishes that appeal to your personal tastes and suit the time and ingredients you have available. If you want to make two courses – say a soup and a main course, a soup and a salad, a main course and a dessert, or a salad and a starter – make sure that they dovetail with each other, so that while one is cooking the other can be prepared. As a general rule, soups and dishes containing chicken, grains and/or vegetables should be put on to cook first, and cold dishes made last. Read the recipe right through before you start cooking and plan your schedule accordingly. While a dish is simmering on top of the stove or baking in the oven it does not need to be supervised, so you could use the time to prepare another dish or clear up, lay the table and so on.

If you are entertaining, remember that one excellent dish made of good-quality ingredients is better than three or four rushed dishes. If you like, you can keep things simple by complementing the main course with easy dishes for which no recipe is required. Dessert can be a simple bowl of fresh fruit, or two or three varieties of exotic fruit, or a cheese board and good bread or biscuits. A few expensive chocolates and a pot of choice coffee will round the meal off memorably.

In general, balance heavier dishes such as those containing cereals or pulses with lighter, crisper foods such as lightly cooked vegetables or salads. Contrasts in texture – hot and cold, plain and rich – will also add interest to a meal. Unusual seasonings such as spice mixtures, chilli sauce, fish sauce, toasted seeds, seaweed condiments and lime juice add further interest without involving you in extra work.

BUYING, PREPARING AND COOKING FRESH FOODS

Fruit and Vegetables

Buy fresh, good-quality produce from a reliable supplier. Cheap, blemished produce is only good for soups, or perhaps for cooking or puréeing in the case of fruits. Buy fruit and vegetables in season when available, since this is when they are likely to be at their tastiest and cheapest.

Fruit ripens and perishes quickly, so buy only as much as you need. Most vegetables keep quite well in cool, dry, ventilated conditions or in the refrigerator. Polythene-wrapped goods tend to go bad quickly. Puncture the wrapping before storage. Separate any slightly damaged or blemished fruit or vegetables from the rest and use them first.

The very best way to maintain maximum vitamin and mineral content of vegetables is to eat them raw.

Of all foods, vegetables tend to be most prone to loss of vitamins and minerals due to overcooking. Nutrients are lost in the cooking water and/or destroyed by overlong cooking. Wash and prepare vegetables immediately before cooking, then either boil them quickly in a small amount of water or steam them. If you do not have a steamer, a metal colander, placed inside a pan with a tight-fitting lid, over an inch or so of water works well. For leaf vegetables such as spinach, wash the leaves well, shake off excess water and cook without any additional water over a moderate heat in a covered pan. In this way you effectively steam the vegetable in its own moisture. Stir-frying is another good method of preserving the flavour and nutritional value of vegetables. It is also a quick and versatile method of making a one-pot meal. Bite-sized pieces of chicken or tofu, for instance, could be added to the vegetables in the pan and just heated through before serving. Cooked grains can also be stirred in at the end. A wok is the best pan to use for stir-frying because its shape concentrates the heat on the food and cooks it evenly and quickly (as long as you stir continuously). Chop the vegetables into bite-sized pieces and add them to the wok according to how long they take to cook. For example, add carrots before courgettes and courgettes before beansprouts.

Pressure-cooking vegetables preserves minerals but the high temperatures used may destroy some vitamins.

Raw Foods

Many studies have been published in recent years that confirm the importance of raw foods for the maintenance of good health and for the healing and prevention of disease. Raw foods contain all their original nutrients and are usually high in fibre. Cooking food always partly destroys some vitamins and the enzymes essential to good digestion, and in some cases it causes loss of minerals, which leach into the cooking water.

Essential raw foods include seeds, nuts, vegetables and fruit. Wherever possible, you should eat unprocessed, unrefined, whole foods. Ideally they should be grown locally by organic farming methods and eaten seasonally.

Seeds and nuts are always at their best either raw or sprouted. Sprouts are cheap, quick to grow and available all year round. They are a particularly rich source of vitamin C and can be used fresh in salads and sandwiches. All that is needed to grow them is a dark, warm place, a jar and some seeds.

To sprout beans, grains or seeds (general method):
Place 1–2 oz (25–50g) of beans, grains or seeds on the bottom of a large wide jar and half-fill it with water. The sprouts will be 6 times as bulky as the unsprouted beans, so make sure the jar is large enough – 1 oz (25g) beans will make approximately 8 oz (225g) beansprouts. Leave them to soak overnight and then drain the water away. Rinse the beans and drain again. A piece of cheesecloth placed over the mouth of the jar makes this job easy.

Now place the jar in a warm, dark place – about 70°F (20°C). Repeat the rinse and drain procedure 3 times a day for 3–5 days. The length of time before the sprouts are ready depends on the bean used and upon the stage at which you decide to harvest them. After this time mung beansprouts will be about 2 in (5cm) long, while sprouts from chickpeas, lentils, kidney beans and soya beans will be ½ in (1cm) long.

Spread the beansprouts (drained) on a tray in the daylight (indoors) for 2–3 hours. They can now be used as required. Store unused beansprouts in a covered container in the refrigerator and rinse before serving. They can be used fresh for up to 3 days or cooked for up to 5 days after harvesting.

If you have two jars available for bean sprouting you will have a constant source of fresh beansprouts available. Scald used cloths and jars before re-using to avoid spoiling the next batch.

Suggestions for Sprouting
(approximate amount to use per batch)

Legumes	Grains	Seeds
4 oz (100g)	*3 tablespoons*	*(see each seed)*
Aduki beans	Barley	Alfalfa *(1 tablespoon)*
Broad beans	Corn	Fenugreek *(3 tablespoons)*
Chickpeas	Millet	Sesame *(3 tablespoons)*
Haricot beans	Oats	Sunflower *(6 tablespoons)*
Kidney beans	Rice	
Lentils	Rye	
Mung beans	Wheat	

Raw vegetables are an important source of minerals, vitamins, enzymes and fibre, and most green vegetables also contain small amounts of complete proteins of the highest biological value. Raw vegetables eaten at the beginning of a meal stimulate both the appetite and the production of enzymes, which later help the digestion of cooked foods. Raw vegetables are also bulky and they thus reduce the quantity of food we wish to eat (without in anyway upsetting the appetite or the pleasure of eating). A green salad after a meal in the French fashion cleans and refreshes the palate.

Herbs, spices and strongly flavoured vegetables such as garlic and onion will promote good health in their own right and they are very useful for adding flavour to other vegetables and raw foods.

One way of using raw vegetables to add flavour and goodness to your diet is to eat pickles. The best type are the salted, pressed variety, such as sauerkraut, popular in northern European countries, Japan and China. Pickling foods in this way is essentially fermenting them, and this not only preserves the vegetables but in some respects increases their nutritive value. This is also the case with the fermented soya bean products, shoyu (soya sauce) and miso (see page 14).

Raw fruit makes the perfect snack, and freshly pressed fruit juices are a convenient way of obtaining nutrients in a concentrated form. Fruit is easily digested, and it also has a cleansing effect on the blood. Like vegetables, fruit is an excellent source of minerals, vitamins, fibre and enzymes. In fact, it is a combination of vitamin C, fibre and enzymes that gives fruit its cleansing properties. To benefit the most from fresh fruit, eat it raw and in season. Organically grown, unsulphured dried fruits are a good substitute. Fruit salads are an interesting way of eating raw fruit and the range of salads is limited only by your imagination and what is available. In hot weather the juiciness and sweetness of the naturally occurring sugars in fruits are most refreshing, and much better for you than a can of fizzy drink.

Raw Juices

Raw juices have a cleansing and detoxifying effect. They are rich in vitamins and minerals, enzymes and natural sugars, and they are easily assimilated into the bloodstream. The best juices are those freshly made in your own juicer. There are three types of electric juicer available. The first is an attachment to a food processor; it works well and, if you already own a food processor, it is the cheapest. The second is an electric juicer in which the residual pulp from the fruit or vegetable remains in the juicing chamber from which the juice is poured. It is perfectly satisfactory but you have to clean it out between each operation. The third and most expensive is an electric juicer that separates the pulp into one container while the juice flows into another. This is the best type if you plan to make a lot of juices, but some of the juice is lost with the pulp.

Only fresh, ripe fruit and vegetables should be made into juice. It is best to use organically grown produce, if available. Wash the produce thoroughly, and make only as much juice as you immediately need, since its goodness disappears rapidly due to oxidation. The following combinations are good both nutritionally and tastewise: carrot and celery, carrot and tomato, orange and pineapple, pineapple and papaya, orange and spinach, orange and grapefruit.

Grains

Grains are the edible seeds of cereals. They are literally embryonic plants and as such are small packages of nourishment and energy. The main grains we eat in the West are rice, wheat (mainly as flour in bread, pasta and so on, but also as bulgar wheat and couscous), barley, oats, millet and buckwheat.

Purchase grains from a reputable and busy health- or wholefood store to ensure they have not been kept for an overlong period. At home, store grains in airtight containers in a cool, dry place. If possible, buy organically grown grains and ensure that they are whole and unrefined.

All grains are very good cooked on their own in water and then served as a side dish to vegetables or with a sauce, or combined with raw vegetables and made into a salad. Cooked grains can also be mixed with other ingredients and baked, or used to stuff vegetables or make rissoles. Some grains benefit from dry-roasting before being boiled in water. This is particularly the case with buckwheat (kasha).

To dry-roast or toast grains, heat them in a dry frying pan or saucepan over a moderate heat, stirring and shaking them until they brown lightly.

The general rules for cooking grains are as follows. Rinse the grain under the cold water tap and drain. Measure the cooking water into the pot and bring it to the boil. Add the grain, stir, add salt if you wish (¼–½ teaspoon per 8 oz/225g grain), and return the pot to the boil. Reduce the heat to very low. Cover the pot and cook until the grain is tender and the water has been absorbed. Cooking times and water-to-grain ratios are given in the table overleaf.

Pasta

Pasta is one of the few foods that combines all the qualities of versatility, nutritiousness, economy and ease of cooking. It is made from a dough of flour and water, and sometimes egg. This is rolled out and then cut into any of a huge variety of shapes before drying and cooking in water. Even most commercial brands of pasta are free of preservatives, other additives and artificial flavourings. The best pasta is made from durum wheat, a 'hard' high-protein variety which gives it body. The gluten protein in durum, unlike that in softer wheats, is resistant to breakdown in water, and pasta made from this variety is easier to cook, less likely to stick to itself and gives that slight bite (*al dente*) which is the mark of

Grain	Water-to-grain ratio	Cooking time	Comments
Barley (whole)	3:1	1 hour	Cooked whole barley can be used like rice. Pearl barley is suitable only for soups and puddings.
Buckwheat	2:1	15–20 minutes	Better known as kasha, which is roasted buckwheat. It is the seed of a herbaceous plant and not truly a grain.
Bulgar wheat	2:1	15–20 minutes	Also known as burghul, prepared by parboiling wholewheat grains, drying and cracking them. Contains all the goodness of wholewheat. Good, dry-roasted before boiling.
Millet	3:1	40–45 minutes	Light yellow millet with small spherical grains can be used in place of rice. Often enjoyed by children more than rice. Nutritionally balanced.
Rice – white	2:1	15–20 minutes	Rice is the world's most important food crop.
– brown	2:1	50–60 minutes	Brown rice is excellent nutritionally, although white rice is more favoured since it is less chewy and cooks more quickly. Long and medium grain rice are best for savoury dishes. Short grain rice is stickier and better for puddings.
Wholewheat berries	3:1	1½–2 hours	Take a lot of cooking, remain quite fibrous but are tasty and filling. Make good salads.
Cracked wheat	2:1	20–25 minutes	Berries are cracked for quicker cooking. Use in place of rice.
Wild rice	3:1	1 hour	Lovely plant grown in fresh water in America, China and Japan. Brown with faint purplish colour when cooked. Delicate, nutty flavour.

perfectly cooked pasta. Pasta is well-balanced nutritionally and the starch contained in it is released into the body at a slow and steady rate – hence its popularity with marathon runners and other athletes in stamina-based sports.

There are many good brands of dried pasta available in the shops. When deciding on the type of pasta to serve with a particular sauce, the usual rule is thick pastas with spicy sauces and thin pastas with something more delicate. Homemade pasta is delicious served on its own with a little melted butter or olive oil and freshly milled black pepper.

Plain Cooked Pasta

The important rule when cooking pasta is to use a large pot and plenty of water. Generally 1 lb (450g) pasta needs 6 pints (3 litres) water. For salt, 1½ tablespoons per 1 lb (450g) pasta is an average amount, added to the pot after the water has boiled and before the pasta is put in. To prevent the pasta sticking to itself during cooking, a little oil can be added to the water. Thus, bring the water to a rolling boil, add the salt and about 2 tablespoons oil, then carefully feed the pasta into the pot and boil, uncovered, until it is soft on the outside but with a slight resistance at the centre, i.e. *al dente*. Cooking times vary depending on the type of pasta, and whether it is bought or homemade. Bought pasta will have cooking times on the packet. Fresh homemade pasta requires 5–7 minutes (thin pasta strips cook more quickly). As soon as the pasta is cooked, drain it in a colander and serve with a sauce and grated cheese or on its own, dressed with melted butter or olive oil and seasoned with freshly milled black pepper.

Boiled Noodles (Serves 4)

The cooking time depends on the type of noodle, and instructions will normally be given on the packet. Here is a general method.

Bring 6 pints (3 litres) water to the boil, add 1 tablespoon salt, 2 tablespoons vegetable oil and 1 lb (450g) dried noodles and stir gently. Cook the noodles, uncovered, in gently boiling water until they are soft on the outside with a slight resistance at the core, about 5 minutes. Drain the noodles and, if they are not to be used immediately, rinse them under cold running water, then drain them again and stir in a little oil to stop them sticking together. To reheat, pour boiling water over the noodles. To fry, see below.

Fried Noodles

There are two ways of frying noodles: soft-frying in a little oil or deep-frying. In each case the noodles are pre-cooked, drained and cooled before frying.

To soft-fry noodles, heat 2–3 tablespoons oil per 8 oz (225g) cooked noodles in a heavy frying pan. Add the noodles and sauté, stirring constantly, for 4–5 minutes. To deep-fry, separate the cooked noodles into single strands, fill a heavy pan or deep fryer with 3–4 in (7.5–10cm) oil and heat to 350°F (180°C). Drop in the noodles, a handful at a time, and fry until medium brown in colour. Remove with chopsticks and drain on absorbent paper.

Beans

'Beans' is the term generally used to describe the seeds of the plants of the legume family, which includes beans, peas and lentils. When properly cooked, they are a versatile, tasty, economical and nutritious food.

Beans contain two starches which are difficult to digest if they are not broken down before eating. For this reason it is essential that they are soaked and cooked for the correct time before consumption. This particularly applies to kidney beans, which also contain a harmful substance destroyed only by correct cooking. This means that you need to remember to put the beans in to soak well in advance of the meal. The usual soaking time is 12 to 24 hours. Strictly speaking, lentils and split peas do not require soaking, but soaking does not do them any harm and it speeds up the cooking time.

Weigh out the beans you require (8 oz/225g will serve 4 people) and cover with cold water (2 pints/1.1 litres per 8 oz/225g beans). Leave overnight and then cook them in their soaking water. This preserves any vitamins or minerals that would be lost if you drained them and used fresh water. Cook until tender, about 1–2 hours, and add more water if the beans start to dry out. If you leave the beans soaking for longer than 24 hours, they should be drained and covered with fresh water before cooking.

Pressure-cooking dramatically reduces the cooking time of beans once they have been soaked. The chart below gives minimum soaking and cooking time for pressure-cooked beans. Note also that nowadays a good variety of tinned beans, such as red beans and chick peas, is available. They are usually of good quality and very convenient for fast food preparation.

Timetable for Soaking and Pressure-Cooking Beans

	Soaking time (hours)	Cooking time (minutes)
Aduki beans	8	6
Black-eyed beans	8	7
Butter beans	10	10
Chickpeas	12	20
Flageolet beans	8	8
Haricot beans	12	8
Kidney beans	12	10
Brown or green lentils	1	3
Split red lentils	no soaking	2
Mung beans	8	4
Pinto beans	8	8
Split peas	1	3
Soya beans	at least 12	30

Soya Bean Products

Soya beans are the most nutritious of all the pulses. They contain as much high-quality protein as meat and the low fat content is entirely unsaturated. However, the dried beans require a lot of cooking and they are not that delicious to eat. In the West this problem has been overcome by converting the beans into products like TVP (textured vegetable protein), which is then made into meat substitutes. Good arguments can be put forward for this idea, but I prefer the approach of the Chinese and Japanese. For centuries they have been making excellent, wholesome and health-enhancing foods that have their own identity (i.e. do not try to imitate meat) from soya beans, using fermentation and other natural processes. There are four main products: tofu, miso, soya sauce and tempeh.

TOFU

Tofu, also known as bean curd, is made from the liquid extracted from crushed soya beans. It is usually sold in small, square slabs. Cut into cubes and added to soups, vegetables or salads it is delicious. Tofu can also be pressed to make it firm enough for frying and less likely to break up in slow-cooking dishes. Tofu is a low-fat, low-carbohydrate food containing a good amount of protein and the minerals calcium, phosphorus and iron. Stored under water it will keep for 3–4 days in the refrigerator. Silken tofu, a commercial product now on sale, is excellent for creaming. Try it with stewed puréed fruit to make a fool, or as a substitute for cheese in cheesecakes, or even for making vegan ice-creams.

MISO

Miso is a fermented soya bean paste. Rich in protein and vitamins, it is a staple food in many countries in the Far East. Japanese mythology places miso along with rice as a gift from the Gods, and it is recognized as an essential requirement of a healthy diet. Naturally fermented miso will keep indefinitely, and the flavour improves with age. Combined with rice or other grains, it can supply all the essential amino acids, and it is also a good source of vitamin B12, often lacking in a vegetarian diet. If carefully fermented, miso contains enzymes that are helpful to the digestion.

Miso is a remarkably versatile ingredient. It may be used as a base for soups or starters, in a marinade for fish or vegetables, as a dressing with vinegar or lemon for salads or in the stock for stews.

SOYA SAUCE

Soya sauce is an all-purpose seasoning used to highlight the individual flavours of the ingredients in the dish to which it is added. It should not be used to drown the flavour of food. Correctly made, soya sauce is prepared from the liquid residue collected when making miso or from soya beans fermented especially for soya sauce production. It is not related to the artificially flavoured liquid found in many bottles claiming to be soya sauce.

Dairy Products

In the demi-vegetarian diet, dairy products are an important source of protein, minerals, especially calcium and vitamins A, D and B, especially riboflavin (vitamin B2). With the exception of skimmed milk, low-fat cheeses and yogurt, dairy products are also a source of saturated fats and should therefore be eaten in moderation. This applies to butter and to any margarine spreads. Spreads made from vegetable oils are normally higher in polyunsaturated fats than butter, but butter is a natural product without additives and it is better to use it than hardened margarines or some of the soft spreads made from synthetically produced fats.

Cheese is a useful ingredient. It is tasty and versatile and can be served either in cooked dishes or uncooked. There are many varieties of hard and soft cheese, each with its own individual flavour and texture. When cooking with cheese, choose a variety whose texture and taste are appropriate to the dish being prepared. Avoid overcooking cheese or it becomes tough and stringy.

Eggs contain a lot of high-quality protein. They also contain cholesterol, and cholesterol-rich diets have been linked to heart disease. However, in small amounts, cholesterol is an essential nutrient and it is a good idea to include a moderate number of eggs or egg dishes in your diet. Free-range eggs taste better and contain none of the chemicals sometimes present in eggs from battery hens. They cost more, but it is worthwhile buying them if you can find a reliable supplier.

Fish

Fish is a good source of protein, vitamins and minerals and is low in fat. It is also quick to prepare and cook, an extremely versatile food and, of equal importance, a joy to eat.

Fish is classified into three main groups: white fish, in which the oil is found in the liver; oily fish, such as herring, mackerel and tuna, in which the oil is dispersed throughout the flesh; and shellfish. The fat content of white fish is normally less than 5 per cent and sometimes as low as 1 per cent. Even oily fish contains less fat than many cuts of meat and most of the fat is polyunsaturated and thus unlikely to contribute to fat-related disease.

Fishmongers stock a wide selection of each of the three groups of fish, plus a selection of smoked fish. Availability and price depend on the season, the weather and the region. Ask your fishmonger's advice on selecting and preparing fish, and take advantage of the lower price of some species. For instance, instead of cod and haddock you could try coley, pollack or ling. Remember also that, as long as they belong to the same general group, different species of fish are interchangeable in recipes.

White fish are divided into two types: round and flat. Large round fish, such as coley and cod, are usually sold in steaks, cutlets or fillets, which can be skinned if desired. Small round fish, such as whiting and haddock, are sold in fillets and, again, can be skinned. Fishmongers can also clean and trim whole fish for you, if you prefer, removing head, fins and tail ready for cooking.

Larger flat fish, such as halibut and turbot, tend to be sold in fillets and steaks, and are trimmed as required. Small flat fish, such as plaice and lemon sole, are usually sold whole and trimmed, or filleted as required.

The golden rule when cooking fish is to buy the freshest fish available and never overcook it. Fish is naturally tender, and it should be cooked for as short a time as possible. Prolonged cooking not only reduces the vitamin and mineral content but also toughens the fish and impairs the flavour and texture.

Chicken

In recent years the popularity of chicken has increased, while our consumption of red meat has declined. Nowadays chicken is an economical ingredient as well as being a convenient and versatile one. With its high protein and low saturated-fat content, plus moderate amounts of thiamine, riboflavin and nicotinic acid, chicken can make a substantial contribution to a healthy diet. Unfortunately, the health-giving qualities and taste of chicken can be negated by the additive-rich foods the birds are often given and the way they are reared. However, because of consumer pressure, more producers are feeding their birds wholesome food and keeping them in better conditions, and this is a trend we should all support by buying free-range chicken.

When buying fresh poultry, check the sell-by date and make sure the bird is free from bruising or other damage. Fresh whole chickens and fresh chicken portions often carry storage instructions on the pack. If they do not, they should always be kept in the refrigerator and cooked within two days of purchase. If they are in a pack, the seal should be broken.

Ready-cooked chicken should also be refrigerated and eaten within three days or, if stuffed, within two days.

Cooking chicken slowly minimizes nutrient loss and also produces the most tender meat; thus slow roasting or stewing are ideal cooking methods. However, the nutrient loss with other cooking techniques is not large. It is just as important in terms of vitamin and mineral preservation to use any cooking juices or stock that may result from the cooking process.

CHEESE AND CASHEW NUT PÂTÉ

This can also be used as a sandwich filling.

4 oz (100g) cream cheese
4 oz (100g) curd cheese
1 small carrot, peeled and
  grated
1 small eating apple, grated
3 oz (75g) broken cashew
  nuts, roasted and crushed
Salt and freshly ground
  black pepper to taste
½ oz (15g) fresh parsley,
  chopped

Serves 4

Beat the two cheeses together in a bowl. Mix in the grated carrot, grated apple and nuts. Season to taste then stir in the chopped parsley. Cover and refrigerate until required. Serve with toast.

SMOKED FISH MOUSSE WITH FRESH TOMATO SAUCE

Filleted smoked trout, salmon or mackerel all work well in this dish, which looks and tastes much better than the simplicity of preparation might imply.

6 oz (175g) smoked trout
  fillets or other smoked fish
1 tablespoon lime juice
1 teaspoon finely grated lime
  rind
6 fl oz (175ml) Greek yogurt
Dash of tabasco sauce
8 oz (225g) ripe tomatoes,
  skinned and seeded
Salt and freshly ground
  black pepper to taste
Lime twists for garnish

Serves 4

Put the smoked trout, lime juice and rind, yogurt and Tabasco in a blender or a food processor and work until smooth. Transfer to a bowl and chill. Purée the tomatoes in a blender and season to taste. To serve, spread a spoonful of the tomato sauce on each of 4 plates. Place large spoonfuls of fish mousse on top and garnish with lime twists.

CHEESE- AND HAZELNUT-STUFFED CELERY AND DATES

Serve as part of a buffet or as an appetizer.

6 oz (175g) ground hazelnuts
6 oz (175g) cream cheese
6 stalks celery, cut into 2 in (5cm) lengths
16 fresh dates, halved and stoned

Serves 4–6

Mix the ground hazelnuts and cream cheese together in a bowl then fill the celery pieces and date halves with this mixture. Arrange the stuffed celery and dates on plates and serve.

GRILLED SARDINES

Sardines are a good source of vitamins B and D and unsaturated fats. Their small size makes them perfectly suited to grilling. Serve as a starter with lemon wedges and thin slices of toast, or with vegetables as a more substantial dish.

1½ lb (675g) fresh (or frozen and defrosted) sardines, gutted and washed
A little vegetable oil for brushing
4 lemon wedges
Salt and freshly ground black pepper to taste

Serves 4

Preheat the grill to medium high. Line the grill pan with kitchen foil and brush with vegetable oil. Make 2 slashes with a knife in each side of the sardines. Put the fish on top of the foil, season and grill for 3–4 minutes on each side. Serve immediately, with lemon wedges and seasoning.

BAKED PEPPERS

Quartered peppers in three colours are filled with a walnut, garlic and tomato mixture and then baked. Serve a quarter portion of each colour to each person.

1 yellow, 1 red and 1 green
  pepper
2 cloves garlic, crushed
2 large tomatoes, skinned
  and chopped
8 walnuts, roughly chopped
12 black olives
A little olive oil

Serves 4

Preheat the oven to 375°F (190°C, gas mark 5). Quarter the peppers and remove the core and seeds. Place the peppers skin side down in an oiled baking dish. Mix together the garlic, tomatoes and walnuts, and spoon into the pieces of pepper. Top each with an olive and drizzle olive oil over them. Bake in the preheated oven for 25 minutes. Serve warm.

MARINATED MUSHROOM SALAD

The marinade 'cooks' the mushrooms to leave them tender and absolutely delicious.

1 lb (450g) small button
  mushrooms
1 clove garlic
Pinch of salt
3 fl oz (75ml) olive oil
2 fl oz (50ml) wine vinegar
Freshly ground black pepper
  to taste
4 oz (100g) onion, finely
  chopped
1 oz (25g) fresh parsley,
  chopped

Serves 4

Wash and dry the mushrooms. In a bowl, crush the clove of garlic with the salt. Slowly whisk in the oil, then the vinegar. Continue whisking until the mixture turns a good yellow colour. Mix in the black pepper, onion and parsley and lastly the mushrooms. Stir them round to coat them evenly then leave, covered, to marinate for at least an hour. Stir them now and then.

SARDINE, EGG AND TOMATO NESTS

Like a nest of Russian dolls the eggs are stuffed with sardines and the tomato halves are stuffed with the eggs.

2 beef tomatoes
4½ oz (115g) can sardine
  fillets in oil (drained if you
  wish)
4 eggs, hardboiled
Salt and freshly ground
  black pepper to taste
Juice of ½ lemon
4 tablespoons mayonnaise

Serves 4

Cut the tomatoes in half and scoop out the pulp and seeds. Mash the sardine flesh with a fork. Halve the eggs lengthways, scoop out the yolks and add to the sardines. Season and add the lemon juice. Fill the egg whites with the mixture, shaping it neatly. Set each stuffed egg half in a tomato half. Top with the mayonnaise, thinned down with a little hot water.

MUSHROOMS IN MUSTARD AND CHILLI SAUCE

The chilli-hot mustard sauce gives a real kick to the otherwise rather bland button mushrooms.

2 oz (50g) butter
12 oz (350g) button
mushrooms, sliced
3 tablespoons white wine
2 tablespoons Dijon mustard
1–2 dried red chillies, finely
chopped, or 1 teaspoon
hot pepper sauce
Salt to taste

Serves 4

Melt the butter in a large saucepan. Toss in the sliced mushrooms and fry gently for a few minutes. Add the white wine, mustard and chopped chillies or pepper sauce. Stir briskly. Cook for a further 2 minutes then serve hot, with triangles of toast.

GRILLED GOAT'S CHEESE SALAD

The perfect starter for the busy cook. Simple, fast and delicious.

2 small, medium-ripe goat's
  cheeses
Salt and freshly ground
  black pepper to taste
Mixed salad leaves
3 tablespoons olive oil
1 tablespoon cider vinegar

Serves 4

Preheat the grill to high. Cut the cheeses in half and place, cut side up, on a sheet of foil on the grill pan. Season with salt and pepper. Arrange the salad leaves on four plates and dress with the oil and vinegar. Grill the cheeses for 5 minutes or until the tops are golden brown. Lay them on the salad and serve immediately.

TWO-CHEESE AND WALNUT DIP

For a low-fat dip make this recipe with cottage cheese, otherwise use cream cheese. The Parmesan cheese can be replaced by mature Cheddar, and nuts other than walnuts can be used. Try roasted almonds or cashews, for instance.

1 tablespoon olive oil
6 oz (175g) cottage cheese or cream cheese
1 tablespoon freshly grated Parmesan cheese
Salt and freshly ground black pepper to taste
A little milk (optional)
2 tablespoons chopped onion
1 tablespoon chopped fresh parsley
1 oz (25g) walnuts, chopped

Serves 4

Put the olive oil, cottage cheese or cream cheese, Parmesan cheese and seasoning into a blender. Blend until smooth. If the mixture is too thick add a little milk and blend again. Add the onion, parsley and walnuts and pulse the blender briefly to mix them in but not to crush them. The dip should be speckled with bits of walnut, onion and parsley. Turn into a bowl and serve.

POTATO AND YOGURT DIP

This is delicious with a salad of sliced cucumber, tomato or cooked beetroot, sprinkled with lemon juice or wine vinegar.

1½ lb (675g) potatoes, washed but not peeled
8 fl oz (225ml) plain yogurt
1 teaspoon salt
½ teaspoon ground ginger
2 teaspoons dried marjoram or oregano
2–4 spring onions, sliced
3 cloves garlic, finely chopped
3 tablespoons olive oil
A few black olives
A few lettuce leaves

Serves 4

Boil the potatoes until tender. Drain, peel and mash them then transfer to a bowl. Stir in the yogurt. Season with the salt, ginger and herbs, then sprinkle in the spring onions and garlic. Stir in the olive oil until a thick, creamy consistency is reached. Decorate with olives and lettuce leaves and serve with pitta bread or toast.

MISO–TAHINI SPREAD

2 tablespoons tahini
1 tablespoon miso
2 teaspoons lemon juice

Serves 2

Mix together the tahini, miso and lemon juice and serve the mixture spread on wholemeal bread.

CHEESE SPREAD

4 oz (100g) cottage cheese
2 oz (50g) Cheddar cheese, grated
1 stalk celery, finely chopped
1 tablespoon mayonnaise
Pinch of cayenne pepper
Salt and freshly ground black pepper to taste

Serves 4

Put all the ingredients in a bowl and mix well.

VARIATIONS

1. Use finely diced green or red pepper, onion or spring onions instead of, or as well as, the celery.

2. After spreading the cheese spread on bread, top it with slices of eating apple.

GARLIC AND ANCHOVY SPREAD

A very tasty spread, delicious on toast or with French bread.

2 cloves garlic, chopped
2×1½ oz (40g) cans
  anchovy fillets, drained
  and chopped
Freshly ground black pepper
  to taste
6 tablespoons lemon juice
2 tablespoons olive oil

Serves 2

Put the garlic, anchovies and black pepper into a blender and process until the mixture is smooth. Add the oil and lemon juice alternately in small amounts, running the blender slowly all the time. The finished paste should be creamy in texture.

SOUPS

SPANISH PEPPER AND COURGETTE SOUP

This is akin to a hot version of gazpacho. The addition of a few anchovy fillets gives an extra bite.

1 onion, finely sliced
1 tablespoon vegetable oil
2 cloves garlic, crushed
2 green peppers, seeded and chopped
2 courgettes, chopped
14 oz (400g) can chopped tomatoes
3 anchovy fillets, chopped
2 tablespoons finely chopped fresh parsley, plus a few sprigs for garnish
1 teaspoon capers
1¼ pints (700ml) vegetable or chicken stock (use stock cubes if you wish)
Salt and freshly ground black pepper to taste

Serves 4

In a large pan sauté the onion in the oil until softened. Add the garlic, peppers and courgettes and sauté for another 3–4 minutes, stirring constantly. Add all the remaining ingredients (except the parsley sprigs) and bring to the boil. Cover and simmer for 20 minutes. Blend until smooth in a blender or food processor. Reheat, and adjust the seasoning if needed. Serve garnished with the sprigs of parsley.

BEAN SOUP

Here's a warmly satisfying soup. It can be made in minutes, too!

2×14 oz (400g) cans
   cannellini (white kidney)
   beans, drained
2 cloves garlic, crushed
½ pint (275ml) vegetable
   stock
2 tesapoons pesto
Salt and freshly ground
   black pepper to taste
Squeeze of lemon juice
½ oz (15g) fresh parsley,
   chopped

Serves 4

Put three-quarters of the drained beans, the garlic and the stock into a blender and process for 1–2 minutes until smooth. Pour the bean purée into a saucepan. Add the pesto and heat gently, stirring all the while. Add a little more water if the soup seems too thick. When the soup is hot, add the reserved beans and season. Continue stirring until the beans are heated through. Add a squeeze of lemon juice and stir in the parsley just before serving.

AVOCADO CREAM SOUP

This subtle, pale green soup makes an unusual way of eating avocados.

2 ripe avocados, peeled,
   stoned and roughly
   chopped
½ pint (275ml) single cream
2 tablespoons dry white
   wine
1½ pints (825ml) vegetable
   stock
Salt and freshly ground
   black pepper to taste
Roughly chopped fresh
   parsley or coriander leaves
   for garnish

Serves 4

Purée the avocado flesh in a blender with the cream and white wine. Bring the vegetable stock to a good rolling boil in a large saucepan. Pour the avocado cream into the stock in a thin, steady stream, stirring all the while. Season to taste. Serve hot, garnished with the herb of your choice.

STILTON AND CELERY SOUP

The distinctive flavour of Stilton blends well with celery. This is a rich and filling soup perhaps best saved for the occasional special meal or for the Christmas period.

2 tablespoons vegetable oil
4 oz (100g) onion, finely chopped
1 lb (450g) celery, chopped
2 pints (1.1 litres) vegetable stock
2 bay leaves
1 lb (450g) potatoes, peeled and diced
6 oz (175g) Stilton cheese, crumbled
Salt and freshly ground black pepper to taste

Serves 4–6

Heat the oil in a large saucepan and gently fry the onion and celery for about 10 minutes. Add the stock, bay leaves and potatoes, bring to the boil, cover and simmer for about 15 minutes until the vegetables are tender. Allow to cool a little, then remove the bay leaves, pour the soup into a blender and process until smooth. Return the soup to the saucepan, add the cheese and heat through gently, stirring, until the cheese has melted. Do not let the soup boil once the cheese has been added. Season to taste and serve.

BEETROOT SOUP

This soup is a glorious colour. The soured cream offsets the sweetness of the beetroot and it can be served either chilled or hot.

1 lb (450g) raw beetroot, peeled and coarsely grated
1 pint (550ml) vegetable stock
Juice of ½ lemon
1 teaspoon caster sugar
Salt and freshly ground black pepper to taste
4 tablespoons soured cream

Serves 4

Put the grated beetroot, stock, lemon juice and sugar into a saucepan. Bring to the boil, cover and simmer for 10–15 minutes, or until the beetroot is tender. Allow to cool, then process until smooth in a blender. Return the soup to the saucepan and reheat. Season to taste. Pour into bowls and serve with the soured cream swirled in.

PUMPKIN AND SWEET POTATO SOUP

The orange of the pumpkin, red of the peppers and faint red blush of·the sweet potatoes delightfully complement one another in this autumnal soup.

1¼ pints (700ml) vegetable or chicken stock
1 lb (450g) orange-flecked pumpkin, skinned, seeded, and cut into 1 in (2.5cm) cubes
3 red peppers, seeded and cut into 1 in (2.5cm) squares
12 oz (350g) sweet potatoes, scrubbed but not peeled, thickly sliced, and each slice quartered
Salt and freshly ground black pepper to taste
8 fl oz (225ml) plain yogurt

Serves 4

Heat the stock in a large pan and add the pumpkin, red peppers (reserve and finely chop a few pieces for garnish) and sweet potatoes. Bring to the boil then reduce the heat, cover and simmer for 30 minutes or until all the vegetables are tender. Remove the pan from the heat and season to taste with salt and black pepper. Stir in all but a tablespoonful of the yogurt. Reheat the soup until it is almost boiling, then transfer to a tureen or individual soup bowls. Garnish with a swirl of yogurt and a little finely chopped red pepper then serve.

BLACKBERRY AND PORT SOUP

An unusual first course at an autumn dinner. Serve hot or chilled.

1 lb (450g) blackberries,
  picked over and rinsed
1½ pints (825ml) water
1 bay leaf
2 in (5cm) stick cinnamon
6 cloves
A few blades mace
A few black peppercorns
1 tablespoon clear honey
3 tablespoons port
1 tablespoon arrowroot
¼ pint (150ml) single cream

Serves 4

Put the blackberries into a pan with the water, bay leaf, spices and honey. Bring to the boil, stirring occasionally, and simmer for 10 minutes. Sieve the soup, then return it to the pan with the port. Heat gently for a few minutes then stir in the arrowroot, dissolved in a few tablespoons of water, and the cream. Continue stirring until the soup thickens, then serve hot or chilled.

CARROT AND OATMEAL SOUP

A surprisingly flavoursome soup made from two staple ingredients.

2 tablespoons vegetable oil
1 large onion, chopped
1 small clove garlic, crushed
2 teaspoons fresh rosemary, chopped, or 1 teaspoon dried rosemary
1 lb (450g) carrots, scrubbed and finely chopped
½ teaspoon curry powder
2 pints (1.1 litres) water
1 level tablespoon medium oatmeal
Sea salt to taste

Serves 4–6

Heat the oil in a saucepan and sauté the onion, garlic and rosemary for 5 minutes. Add the carrots and curry powder, pour in with the water, stir well and bring to the boil. Add the oatmeal and cook, covered, over a medium heat, stirring occasionally, until the carrots are soft, about 15 minutes. Liquidize the soup in a blender, add salt to taste, and serve. Add more boiling water to the blender for a thinner soup.

VEGETABLE SOUP WITH RICE FLOUR DUMPLINGS

Rice flour dumplings are easy to make and they add substance to this soup, which has a flavour of the Far East.

2 tablespoons vegetable oil
8 oz (225g) white radish (daikon) or baby turnips, peeled and diced
2 or 3 Chinese cabbage leaves or other leafy vegetable, coarsely shredded
1¾ pints (1 litre) vegetable or chicken stock
8 oz (225g) rice flour
About ¼ pint (150ml) boiling water
Salt to taste
Sprigs of fresh parsley, mint or coriander for garnish

Serves 4

Heat the oil in a large saucepan and sauté the white radish or turnips until softened. Add the Chinese cabbage and stock and bring to the boil. Reduce the heat, cover and simmer for 20 minutes. While the soup is cooking, prepare the rice flour dumplings: put the rice flour in a bowl and pour in the boiling water while stirring vigorously with a wooden spoon. Add only as much water as necessary to produce a fairly stiff dough. Knead the dough for 3–4 minutes, then break off small portions and roll them into dumplings. Season the soup with salt and drop in the dumplings. Initially they will drop to the bottom of the pan, but as they cook through (2–3 minutes) they will rise to the surface. Serve the soup garnished with sprigs of fresh herbs.

FENNEL SOUP

Fennel is loved by some and disliked by others. Certainly it has a strong flavour of aniseed but this becomes more subtle with cooking. For those who enjoy a strong aniseed taste, a little Pernod may be added to the soup.

2 oz (50g) butter
4 oz (100g) onion, thinly sliced
1 clove garlic, crushed
4 oz (100g) carrot, peeled and sliced
4 small fennel bulbs, sliced (discard the woody top stalks but reserve a few fronds for garnish)
1½ pints (825ml) chicken or vegetable stock
1 bouquet garni
Salt and freshly ground black pepper to taste
2 egg yolks
Juice of 1 lemon
1 teaspoon Pernod (optional)
4 thin lemon slices

Serves 4

Melt the butter in a large saucepan. Add the onion and garlic and cook gently for 5 minutes. Add the sliced carrot and fennel and cook for another 5 minutes. Add the stock, bouquet garni and salt and pepper to taste. Bring to the boil, cover and simmer for 20 minutes until the vegetables are very tender. Remove the bouquet garni and cool the soup slightly. Process in a blender until smooth, then return the soup to the pan and reheat. Just before serving, whisk the egg yolks and lemon juice together then add a ladleful of the soup. Keep whisking until smooth, then add this mixture to the soup a little at a time. Taste, and add more lemon juice if needed. To bring out the fennel flavour add the Pernod, if using. Pour the soup into 4 bowls and float a lemon slice on each one, with a few fennel fronds.

CREAM OF SWEETCORN SOUP

Thick and creamy with a delicious taste and colour

2 oz (50g) butter
4 oz (100g) onion, finely
  chopped
6 oz (175g) potatoes, peeled
  and diced
Salt and freshly ground
  black pepper to taste
½ oz (15g) plain flour
1 pint (550ml) milk
½ pint (275ml) chicken or
  vegetable stock
2×11 oz (300g) cans
  sweetcorn, drained
2 tablespoons Greek yogurt

Serves 4

Melt the butter in a saucepan, add the onion and cook gently for 5 minutes. Add the diced potatoes and cook for a further 3 minutes. Season. Stir in the flour and then gradually add the milk and stock, stirring constantly. Bring to the boil. Add half the sweetcorn, cover and simmer for 20 minutes. Allow to cool a little, then process in a blender until smooth. Return the soup to the heat, add the remaining sweetcorn and warm it through. Pour into 4 warmed bowls and add a dollop of yogurt to each bowl.

TOMATO SOUP

This is a flavoursome mildly sweet-sour soup that is filling and nutritious.

2 tablespoons vegetable oil
1 large onion, chopped
1 teaspoon dried basil
1 bay leaf
1 tablespoon wholemeal flour
1 small carrot, scrubbed and finely chopped
1 stalk celery, finely chopped
1 teaspoon honey or brown sugar
1 tablespoon cider vinegar
14 oz (400g) can chopped tomatoes
1 pint (550ml) water
1 clove garlic, crushed
Soya sauce to taste
Salt to taste
2 fl oz (50ml) milk
2 tablespoons toasted sunflower seeds for garnish

Serves 4

Heat the oil in a pan and sauté the onion, basil and bay leaf for 2 minutes. Stir in the flour. Add the carrot, celery, honey or sugar, cider vinegar, tomatoes and water. Bring to the boil, reduce the heat, cover and cook for 15–20 minutes, until the vegetables are soft. Liquidize the soup in a blender with the garlic, soya sauce and salt. Return the soup to the pan, add the milk and reheat gently. Serve with a sprinkling of toasted sunflower seeds.

WATERCRESS SOUP

Watercress soup is quick and easy to make, and it also freezes well. The crunchiness of the toasted almonds makes a good garnish.

1 tablespoon vegetable oil
4 oz (100g) onion, finely
  chopped
6 oz (175g) watercress,
  washed and trimmed
¾ pint (450ml) vegetable
  stock
½ pint (275ml) milk
Salt and freshly ground
  black pepper to taste
1 oz (25g) flaked almonds,
  toasted

Serves 4

Heat the oil in a saucepan. Add the onion and fry gently until softened. Add the watercress and stock. Bring to the boil, cover and simmer for 5 minutes. Allow to cool slightly, then process in a blender until smooth. Return the soup to the saucepan, add the milk and heat through gently. Season to taste. Serve the soup sprinkled with the toasted almonds.

CHILLED MELON AND SWEET WHITE WINE SOUP

This is a good soup to make with cantaloupe or Charentais melons. It doesn't matter if the melon is rather overripe (the stage at which your greengrocer may be selling it cheaply). The quantities given below are approximate and will depend to some degree on the sweetness of the melon.

1¼ lbs (550g) melon flesh (about 2 lb/900g melon), chopped
3 fl oz (75ml) sweet white wine
Juice of ½ lemon
Salt and freshly ground black pepper to taste
Finely chopped fresh mint for garnish

Serves 4

Purée the melon flesh in a blender. Pour into a bowl, stir in the wine and lemon juice and season lightly with salt and black pepper. Chill for 30 minutes. Adjust the seasoning if needed, garnish with fresh mint and serve.

CHILLED TOMATO AND YOGURT SOUP

A pale pink summer soup that is easy to make and refreshing to eat.

2×14 oz (400g) cans
  tomatoes
½ pint (275ml) plain yogurt
1 clove garlic, crushed to a
  smooth paste with a little
  salt
½ cucumber, peeled and
  finely diced
½ oz (15g) fresh chives,
  chopped
Salt and freshly ground
  black pepper to taste

Serves 4

Put the tomatoes, yogurt and garlic into a blender and process for 1–2 minutes. Pour into a bowl. Stir in the cucumber and most of the chopped chives and season to taste. Chill for 2 hours. Garnish with the remaining chives and serve.

SALADS

TURKISH BULGAR WHEAT SALAD

Bulgar wheat is a most convenient ingredient. Pour hot water over it, leave for 15 minutes and it's cooked. Serve this salad as a side dish, or with crusty bread or warmed pitta bread and cucumber slices in minted yogurt for a light meal.

6 oz (175g) bulgar wheat
¼ pint (150ml) boiling water
1 onion, finely diced
4 firm tomatoes, quartered
1 red pepper, seeded and
    chopped
1 tablespoon finely chopped
    fresh parsley
2 tablespoons lemon juice
2 tablespoons olive oil
Salt and freshly ground
    black pepper to taste

Serves 4

Put the bulgar wheat in a serving bowl. Pour over the water, stirring all the time. Cover and set aside for 15 minutes. Stir the onion, tomatoes and red pepper into the bulgar wheat. Add the parsley, lemon juice, olive oil and seasoning. Combine thoroughly and serve.

FRUIT AND CHEESE SALAD

A big salad with lots of colour and texture. A meal by itself.

1 apple, cored and finely
  chopped
1 pear, cored and finely
  chopped
Juice of a lemon
2 stalks celery, finely
  chopped
4 oz (100g) small green or
  black grapes
2 oz (50g) mixed nuts,
  chopped
2 oz (50g) Gouda, cut into
  thin strips
2 oz (50g) Edam, cut into
  thin strips
2 spring onions, finely
  chopped
1 Ogen, Charentais or
  canteloupe melon, peeled,
  seeded and finely sliced
7 oz (200g) cottage cheese
  (with pineapple if you
  wish)

DRESSING
2 tablespoons orange juice
1 teaspoon cider vinegar
1 teaspoon French mustard
Salt and freshly ground
  black pepper to taste

Serves 4

Put the chopped apple and pear in a large salad bowl and sprinkle with the lemon juice. Add the celery, grapes and nuts. Whisk the ingredients for the dressing together and add just enough to the fruit and nut mixture to bind it. Mix the Gouda and Edam with the spring onions and moisten with a little dressing. Arrange the melon slices on a large, oval plate. In the centre, make a little mound of the cottage cheese. Spoon the fruit and nut salad around this. Scatter the cheese and spring onions over the top of the salad.

HERRING SALAD

This simple version of a German classic is creamy and subtle. It is good either as an hors d'oeuvre or a snack lunch.

2 jars of pickled herring
   fillets cut into 1 in (2.5cm)
   thick strips
8 oz (225g) cooked beetroot,
   cut into ½ in (1.25cm)
   cubes
4 oz (100g) onion, very
   thinly sliced
1 gherkin, chopped
1 tablespoon cider vinegar
3 tablespoons plain yogurt
3 tablespoons good
   mayonnaise
Salt and freshly ground
   black pepper to taste

Serves 4

Toss the herring slices, beetroot cubes, onion rings and gherkin together in a bowl. Sprinkle the cider vinegar on top. Mix the yogurt, mayonnaise and salt and black pepper together well. Stir into the salad and toss again thoroughly.

CHICKPEA SALAD IN LEMON DRESSING

A quick and filling salad. Serve for a summer lunch with a light salad and bread. In the winter serve as a side dish to a rice or other grain meal.

2 tablespoons olive oil
2 tablespoons lemon juice
1 small onion, finely chopped
2 cloves garlic, crushed
3 tablespoons chopped fresh chives
Sea salt to taste
14 oz (400g) can chickpeas, drained

Serves 3-4

Mix the olive oil with the lemon juice in a bowl and beat well. Add the onion, garlic, chives and sea salt. Toss the chickpeas in this dressing and serve.

PEAR, CUCUMBER AND GRAPE SALAD

This unusual salad makes a good side dish for a meal with cheese in it or simply as an accompaniment to cheese and bread. Served well chilled, it also makes an appetizing starter. Black grapes are best for this salad but only use them if you have time to remove the pips. Otherwise, small green seedless grapes are fine.

3 ripe but firm pears
½ cucumber
4 oz (100g) black grapes, seeded, or green seedless grapes

DRESSING
4 fl oz (100ml) vegetable oil
2 tablespoons wine vinegar or cider vinegar
Salt and freshly ground black pepper to taste
1 teaspoon prepared mustard

Serves 4

Peel and core the pears, slice 1 thinly and dice the remaining 2. Cut the piece of cucumber lengthwise in half and scoop out the seeds. Thinly slice a quarter of the cucumber and dice the rest. Make a bed of the pear and cucumber slices in a small salad bowl. Put the remaining diced pear and cucumber and the grapes (reserve 5 grapes) into a separate bowl. Combine the dressing ingredients and mix well. Add the dressing to the diced pear, cucumber and grapes and toss well. Pour this mixture over the bed of pear and cucumber slices. Garnish the salad with the reserved grapes, chill and serve.

WARM LENTIL SALAD

The variety of tinned beans and lentils now available in supermarkets makes salads such as this one easy to prepare for those who do not have the time to soak and cook pulses from scratch. The quality of this salad depends on using a very good olive oil.

1 lb (450g) can whole green or brown lentils/8 oz (225g) dried lentils, cooked until tender and drained
4 tablespoons olive oil (preferably extra virgin)
1 tablespoon cider vinegar
Salt and freshly ground black pepper to taste
2 shallots or 1 small onion, finely chopped
1–2 cloves garlic, crushed

Serves 4–6

Drain the lentils and heat them through in a pan. Turn into a serving bowl and stir in the remaining ingredients. Serve warm or cold.

BROCCOLI AND SUN-DRIED TOMATO SALAD

Sun-dried tomatoes are now widely available in large supermarkets, good delicatessens and health-food stores. They are a useful store cupboard ingredient, and particularly good for adding colour and flavour to salads.

1 lb (450g) broccoli, cut into bite-sized pieces
2 tablespoons olive oil
2 tablespoons sesame seeds
1 clove garlic, crushed
6 sun-dried tomato halves, thinly sliced
Salt and freshly ground black pepper to taste
1 tablespoon lemon juice

Serves 4

Bring a large pan of water to the boil and add the broccoli. Cook for 2–3 minutes, then drain and transfer to a bowl of very cold water for a few minutes to prevent any further cooking. Drain into a colander and set aside. Heat the oil in a frying pan and sprinkle in the sesame seeds. Add the garlic and fry until both the sesame seeds and garlic are just browned. Put the broccoli in a serving dish, mix in the sun-dried tomatoes, then pour over the oil, sesame seeds and garlic. Season with salt and black pepper, sprinkle over the lemon juice and serve.

CHICKEN AND GRUYÈRE SALAD

This salad keeps well and it makes a good dish for a picnic. Any strong cheese can be substituted for the Gruyère.

1 lb (450g) cooked, boned chicken
2 stalks celery, thickly sliced
2 oz (50g) Gruyère cheese, grated
2 oz (50g) black seedless grapes, halved
1 red apple, chopped
4 fl oz (100ml) olive oil
1 tablespoon white wine vinegar
2 tablespoons soured cream
2 tablespoons mayonnaise
2 tablespoons chopped fresh parsley
3 oz (75g) pecan nuts or walnuts, toasted
Salt and freshly ground black pepper to taste

Serves 4

Skin the chicken and cut into large bite-sized pieces. Place the chicken, celery, cheese, grapes and apple in a large bowl. Add all the other ingredients and toss well. Adjust the seasoning, if necessary, cover and chill for 15 minutes before serving.

SOUTH SEA ISLAND FISH SALAD

Although this exotic salad has a lot of ingredients, once they have been collected together it is quick to make. Serve as a main course.

1½ lb (675g) white fish fillets, cooked, skinned and roughly chopped
Juice of 1 lime
Juice of 2 lemons
4 oz (100g) fresh coconut, grated, or 2 oz (50g) desiccated coconut
1 red pepper, seeded and finely chopped
1 green pepper, seeded and finely chopped
2 bananas, thinly sliced
4 tomatoes, chopped
1 cucumber, peeled and diced
4 oz (100g) canned pineapple, drained and chopped
¼ teaspoon ground cumin
1 green chilli, finely chopped
1 clove garlic, crushed
Salt and freshly ground black pepper to taste
¼ pint (150ml) soured cream
2 tablespoons single cream

Serves 6–8

Mix together the fish, lime juice and lemon juice, and leave to marinate in the refrigerator for 1 hour. Drain the fish, reserving 1 tablespoon of the juice. Place the fish, coconut, red pepper, green pepper, bananas, tomatoes, cucumber and pineapple in a large bowl and toss well to mix. Mix together the reserved citrus juice, cumin, chilli, garlic and salt and pepper to form a smooth paste. Gradually stir in the soured cream and the single cream then pour this mixture over the salad. Toss well and serve.

PINEAPPLE, BANANA AND TOFU SALAD

Japan meets the West Indies in this exotic, low-fat starter.

½ fresh pineapple, peeled, cored, cut into rings then diced (or use 8 oz/225g canned pineapple)
3 bananas, sliced
4 oz (100g) tofu, cut into 1 in (2.5cm) cubes
¼ cucumber, cut lengthwise in half then sliced
Clear honey to garnish

Serves 4

Combine all the ingredients in a large bowl. Mix gently, divide between 4 bowls, pour a little honey over each and serve.

POTATO SALAD

A recipe from Germany, where no picnic is complete without its kartoffelsalat.

1 lb (450g) small new
   potatoes
2 tablespoons wine vinegar
1 teaspoon sugar
Salt and freshly ground
   black pepper to taste
4 oz (100g) onion, chopped
1 tablespoon chopped
   gherkin
¼ pint (150ml) good
   mayonnaise
1 hardboiled egg, chopped
A little chopped fresh
   parsley for garnish

Serves 4

Wash the potatoes well, then boil until tender in salted water. Drain and leave to cool. Put the vinegar, sugar and salt and pepper into a large serving bowl and whisk to combine. Add the chopped onion and gherkin and the cooled potatoes (cut up any large potatoes to make them all the same size). Mix in the mayonnaise. Garnish with the chopped hardboiled egg and parsley. Leave at room temperature for 1 hour before serving.

TOFU, GREENS AND PARMESAN SALAD

This culturally confused combination is a main-course salad.
Serve with crusty bread for a light, nourishing and tasty meal.

About 4 tablespoons olive
  oil
8 oz (225g) tofu, cut into ½
  in (1.25cm) cubes
Salt and freshly ground
  black pepper to taste
Juice of 1 lemon
8 oz (225g) broccoli,
  cauliflower or green beans,
  cut into 1 in (2.5cm)
  pieces
1 bunch salad leaves or
  young spinach
1 onion, finely sliced
3–4 tablespoons freshly
  grated Parmesan cheese
1 tablespoon chopped fresh
  dill (optional)
2 cloves garlic, crushed

Serves 4

Heat 1 tablespoon of the oil in a
small frying pan, add the tofu and
fry, turning frequently, until the
cubes are crisp and brown. Sprinkle
with salt and pepper and half the
lemon juice then leave to cool. Put
the broccoli, cauliflower or green
beans in a pan, pour boiling water
over and boil for 2 minutes. Rinse
under cold water, drain and set
aside. Put the salad leaves or spinach
in a large bowl with the onion, tofu,
broccoli or other vegetable,
Parmesan and dill. Spoon in just
enough of the remaining olive oil to
coat all the ingredients lightly when
tossed. Just before serving, mix the
remaining lemon juice with the
garlic and seasoning in a small
bowl. Pour over the salad and toss
well.

CARROT AND WALNUT SALAD

Good with cheese dishes or just cheese and bread

12 oz (350g) firm carrots,
    peeled and grated
2 oz (50g) walnut pieces (or
    other nuts)
Coarsely chopped fresh
    parsley to taste
Salt to taste
1 teaspoon coarsely ground
    black pepper (use a pestle
    and mortar if possible)
1 tablespoon cider vinegar
    or wine vinegar
4 tablespoons vegetable oil

Serves 4–6

Combine all the ingredients in a
bowl and mix well together. Serve.

HARICOT BEAN AND ONION SALAD

The fresh herbs really brighten up the beans. You can substitute any other combination of herbs for the one suggested below. Serve as a part of a light lunch or as a side dish to a cooked vegetable or grain dish.

2 tablespoons olive oil
1 tablespoon lemon juice
Salt and freshly ground
   black pepper to taste
14 oz (400g) can haricot
   beans, drained
2 tablespoons chopped fresh
   parsley
1 tablespoon chopped fresh
   dill
1 tablespoon chopped fresh
   mint
1 large onion, thinly sliced
1 ripe but firm tomato,
   sliced
1 green pepper, seeded and
   sliced

Serves 3–4

In a large serving bowl, whisk together the olive oil, lemon juice, vinegar, salt and black pepper. Add the beans to the bowl and mix together well. Add the herbs, onion, tomato and green pepper, toss well then serve.

GAZPACHO SALAD

An attractive salad, refreshing when served slightly chilled. The ideal accompaniment to any main course.

1 small cucumber, peeled and thinly sliced
4 fl oz (100ml) olive oil
2 tablespoons white wine vinegar
1 clove garlic, crushed
1 teaspoon ground coriander
Salt and freshly ground black pepper to taste
8 oz (225g) button mushrooms
5 spring onions, chopped
1 oz (25g) fresh parsley, chopped
3 ripe tomatoes, cut into wedges
1 green pepper, seeded and cut into strips

Serves 4

Place the cucumber slices in a colander, sprinkle with salt and leave to drain for 20 minutes. Rinse with cold water and dry thoroughly. Meanwhile, in a large bowl make the dressing by beating the olive oil, vinegar, garlic, coriander and salt and pepper together. Add the whole mushrooms, chopped spring onions, cucumber slices and parsley. Toss together gently. Chill in the refrigerator for 1 hour then add the tomato wedges and green pepper strips. Toss all the vegetables together gently and serve at once.

STILTON AND WATERCRESS SALAD

The tangy lemon dressing complements the pepperiness of the watercress and cuts into the strong flavour of the cheese.

2 bunches watercress, washed, drained and trimmed
4 oz (100g) Stilton cheese, crumbled
½ cucumber, peeled and thinly sliced
3 tablespoons lemon juice
3 tablespoons sunflower oil
Salt and freshly ground black pepper to taste

Serves 4

Put the watercress in a salad bowl and add the crumbled cheese and the cucumber slices. Toss together gently. Put the lemon juice, oil and salt and pepper into a small screw-topped jar and shake well until the dressing is creamy and thick. Pour the dressing over the salad and gently toss again. Serve at once.

BROAD BEAN AND RADISH SALAD

The radishes add bright colour and crunchiness to this smooth and creamy salad. It goes well with just about any main course.

1 lb (450g) broad beans
 (shelled weight)
Juice of ½ lemon
1 teaspoon olive oil
1 bunch radishes, trimmed
 and thinly sliced
3 tablespoons plain yogurt
4 tablespoons mayonnaise
1 oz (25g) mixed fresh
 herbs, chopped

Serves 4

Cook the broad beans in boiling salted water for 10 minutes or until tender. Drain and place in a salad bowl. Mix with the lemon juice and the olive oil and leave to cool. When cool, toss in the sliced radishes. Mix together the yogurt, mayonnaise and most of the chopped herbs. Pour this mixture over the vegetables and mix well. Sprinkle over the remaining herbs before serving.

FLAGEOLET BEAN, TOMATO AND OLIVE SALAD

14 oz (400g) can flageolet
   beans, rinsed and
   drained/6 oz (175g) dried
   haricot beans, soaked
   overnight, cooked until
   tender and drained
4 ripe tomatoes, halved,
   seeded and diced
2 oz (50g) button
   mushrooms, thinly sliced
2 oz (50g) black olives,
   stoned and halved
½ oz (15g) fresh parsley,
   chopped
Salt and freshly ground
   black pepper to taste
2 tablespoons olive oil
1 tablespoon lemon juice
1 teaspoon French mustard
1 teaspoon soft brown sugar

Serves 4

Put the flageolet beans, diced tomatoes, sliced mushrooms, olives and parsley into a bowl. Season to taste. Blend the olive oil, lemon juice, mustard and sugar together. Spoon this dressing over the bean mixture and toss together gently. Chill until required.

COURGETTE AND LEEK SALAD

A different sort of green salad. The delicate flavours of young leeks and courgettes make a pleasant accompaniment to a light lunch.

12 oz (350g) courgettes, trimmed and sliced
10 oz (275g) leeks, trimmed and sliced
1 tablespoon chopped parsley
1 tablespoon chopped fresh mint
1 teaspoon chopped fresh chives
3 tablespoons Vinaigrette Dressing (see below)

VINAIGRETTE DRESSING:
2 tablespoons vegetable oil
1 tablespoon cider vinegar or lemon juice
Salt and freshly ground black pepper to taste

Serves 4

Blanch the courgettes in boiling water for 2 minutes. Rinse under cold water, drain and pat dry. Blanch the leeks in boiling water for about 3 minutes. Drain and pat dry. Mix the courgettes and leeks together in a bowl, mix the herbs together and scatter them over the vegetables. Pour the dressing over the vegetables while they are still warm. Toss lightly. Store in the refrigerator until ready to serve.

SPICED POTATO SALAD WITH FRESH CORIANDER LEAVES

A wonderfully flavoursome Indian-inspired potato salad.

1½ lb (675g) small, whole new potatoes, washed or other potato, peeled and chopped
2 tablespoons sesame oil or other vegetable oil
2 oz (50g) sesame seeds
1 tablespoon mustard seeds
1 in (2.5cm) piece fresh ginger root, peeled and finely grated
½ teaspoon chilli powder or hot pepper sauce
Salt to taste
Juice of ½ lemon
2 tablespoons chopped fresh coriander leaves

Serves 4–6

Put the potatoes in a pan with plenty of boiling water and boil them until only just tender. Drain and put them into a salad bowl. Heat the oil in a frying pan and stir in the sesame seeds, mustard seeds, ginger, chilli powder or hot pepper sauce, and salt. Fry over moderate heat, stirring constantly, for 3–4 minutes. Stir the oil and spices into the potatoes, add the lemon juice and mix well. Allow to cool completely and then gently stir in the coriander leaves.

CHILLI-HOT ONION SALAD

For a less sharp-tasting salad, replace the vinegar with plain yogurt.

2 onions, finely sliced
3 tomatoes, chopped
1 small cucumber, chopped
1 green chilli, seeded and
   finely chopped
1 tablespoon chopped fresh
   coriander leaves
½ teaspoon salt
3 tablespoons cider vinegar

Serves 4

Mix the onions, tomatoes, cucumber, chilli and coriander leaves together in a bowl and sprinkle with the salt and vinegar. Leave to stand for 30 minutes before serving.

APPLE AND CHESTNUT SALAD

Out of season, tinned chestnuts are convenient to use and they work well in this recipe; rehydrated diced chestnuts could also be used. Best of all, peeled, precooked vacuum-packed chestnuts are now avaiable in some specialist food shops.

2 eating apples, cored and
  chopped
3 stalks celery, chopped
3 tablespoons chopped
  cooked chestnuts
3 tablespoons olive oil
2 tablespoons wine vinegar
  or cider vinegar
4 oz (100g) crumbled feta
  cheese or to taste
1 teaspoon crushed dried
  marjoram or oregano

Serves 4

Combine the apples, celery and chestnuts in a bowl with the oil and vinegar. Sprinkle over the cheese and dried herbs.

GRAINS, PASTA AND BEANS

BROCCOLI AND MUSHROOM RISOTTO

This is most delicious. You can use different varieties of mushrooms, such as oyster, chestnut or straw mushrooms, if you can get them. Italian Arborio rice should always be used for Italian-style risottos such as this one, and it is now available in most large supermarkets.

2 tablespoons olive oil
8 oz (225g) onions, finely chopped
2 cloves garlic, crushed
12 oz (350g) Arborio rice
12 oz (350g) mushrooms, chopped
12 oz (350g) broccoli, florets diced into ½ in (1.25cm) pieces
¼ pint (150ml) dry white wine
1 pint (550ml) vegetable stock
2 oz (50g) Parmesan cheese, freshly grated
Salt and freshly ground black pepper to taste
Finely chopped fresh parsley for garnish

Serves 4

Heat the oil in a large heavy-based saucepan and fry the onions and garlic until softened but not coloured. Stir in the rice and cook for about 1 minute. Add the mushrooms and broccoli and stir well. Pour in the wine and stir well. In a separate pan, heat the stock until almost boiling. Add the hot stock, 1 ladleful at a time, to the rice, waiting until the liquid is absorbed before adding more. Stir the rice constantly and make sure the liquid is always bubbling. When the rice is cooked but still *al dente* (about 25–30 minutes), add half the Parmesan cheese, stir, and season to taste. Serve on warm plates, garnished with parsley and sprinkled with the rest of the Parmesan.

CARNIVAL RICE, BEANS AND VEGETABLES

The ingredients are simply cooked together in coconut milk (now available canned) to produce a nutritious one-pot meal.

8 oz (225g) long grain
  brown rice
½ pint (275ml) coconut
  milk
8 oz (225g) cooked kidney
  beans (canned are fine)
2 carrots, thickly sliced
1 onion, sliced
8 oz (225g) pumpkin,
  peeled, seeded and
  roughly chopped
Salt and freshly ground
  black pepper to taste

Serves 4

Put all the ingredients into a large pan and add water just to cover. Bring slowly to the boil. Cover, reduce the heat and simmer for 30 minutes or until the rice is tender. Check the water level from time to time. Ideally all the liquid should be just absorbed at the end of the cooking period.

CARIBBEAN RICE

12oz (350g) easy-cook
  brown rice
3 tablespoons sunflower oil
1 lb (450g) onions, chopped
2 cloves garlic, crushed
2 in (5cm) piece fresh ginger
  root, peeled and grated
1 eating apple, chopped
4 courgettes, sliced
1 red pepper, diced
4 tomatoes, diced
1 oz (25g) raisins
2 bananas, sliced
1 tablespoon tomato purée
14 oz (400g) can pineapple
  chunks, drained
1 tablespoon soya sauce
Yogurt for garnish

Serves 4

Cook the rice according to the instructions on the packet. Drain, rinse well in cold water and drain again. While the rice is cooking, heat the oil in a large pan and fry the onions, garlic, ginger, apple, courgettes, red pepper, tomatoes and raisins. When tender, add the bananas, tomato purée and drained pineapple chunks. Add the cooked, drained rice and the soya sauce and stir gently until the rice is heated through. Serve in bowls, topped with yogurt.

TABBOULEH WITH SMOKED FISH AND CHILLIES

Bulgar wheat is quick and convenient to prepare. Combined here with smoked fish and chillies it provides a nutritious and spicy one-dish meal.

8 oz (225g) bulgar wheat
1 small onion, finely
    chopped
Juice of 2 lemons
1–2 fresh green chillies,
    seeded and finely chopped
1 pair boneless kippers (or
    other smoked fish),
    skinned and flaked
3 tablespoons coarsely
    chopped fresh mint leaves
3 tablespoons olive oil
Lemon wedges to garnish

Serves 4

Put the bulgar wheat in a bowl, pour boiling water over and leave to stand for 15 minutes. Drain, then stir in the onion, lemon juice, chillies and flaked fish. Stir in the chopped mint and the olive oil, garnish with lemon wedges and serve.

JAMBALAYA

This is a very popular Creole rice dish, similar to a Spanish paella.

2 tablespoons olive oil
8 oz (225g) raw chicken, cut into ½ in (1.25cm) chunks
1 onion, finely chopped
1 large clove garlic, crushed
2 stalks celery, finely chopped
2 teaspoons grated fresh ginger root
1 small green pepper, seeded and finely sliced
8 oz (225g) long grain brown rice, soaked in water for 2 hours then drained
1 pint (550ml) chicken stock
7 oz (200g) cooked pinto or haricot beans, drained (canned are fine)
4 oz (100g) peeled prawns (optional)
7 oz (200g) can chopped tomatoes
1 tablespoon lemon juice and a thin curl of lemon rind
1 teaspoon paprika or half paprika and half cayenne pepper
Freshly ground black pepper to taste
4 allspice berries, crushed

Serves 4–5

Heat the oil in a pan and stir-fry the chicken pieces until brown. Remove the chicken from the pan and set aside. In the same pan, sauté the onion, garlic and celery for 4 minutes. Add the ginger and green pepper and fry for a further 2 minutes. Now add the well-drained rice and fry for 5 minutes so that it becomes well coated with juices. Add all the remaining ingredients, including the chicken, to the pan. Bring to the boil then simmer, tightly covered, for 20–25 minutes until all the liquid has been absorbed and the rice is tender.

ITALIAN BAKED RICE

Once the rice is cooked (and extra could be made at a previous meal with this dish in mind) this casserole is very quick to put together. The finished dish is surprisingly good for such simple preparation and ingredients. Serve with a lettuce and tomato salad.

1½ lb (675g) cooked brown or white rice
½ teaspoon black pepper
2 teaspoons salt
4 oz (100g) tomato purée
8 fl oz (225g) vegetable stock or water
1 green pepper, seeded and diced
8 oz (225g) cheese, grated
4 oz (100g) fresh brown breadcrumbs
2 oz (50g) butter

Serves 4–6

Preheat the oven to 350°F (180°C, gas mark 4). Combine all the ingredients except the breadcrumbs and butter. Turn the mixture into a lightly greased casserole dish. Cover with the breadcrumbs and dot the top with the butter. Bake in the preheated oven for 30 minutes or until well browned.

HIGHLAND OAT SQUARES

These savoury oat squares are especially popular with children. If you wish, serve them with fresh vegetables and/or a salad.

2 oz (50g) butter
1 onion, finely chopped
4 oz (100g) mushrooms, chopped
5 oz (150g) rolled oats
6 oz (175g) carrot, finely grated
5 oz (150g) cheese, grated
1 egg, beaten
1 clove garlic, crushed (optional)
1 tablespoon soya sauce
1 tablespoon tomato sauce or tomato purée
1 teaspoon dried basil
Salt and freshly ground black pepper to taste

Makes 9×3 in (7.5cm) squares

Preheat the oven to 325°F (175°C, gas mark 3). Melt the butter in a pan and gently cook the onion and mushrooms in it for 5 minutes. Transfer to a mixing bowl, add all the other ingredients and mix well. Press the mixture into a greased, shallow baking tin about 9 in (23cm) square and bake for 25–30 minutes until browned. Cut into 9 squares. Serve hot or cold.

QUICK ALMOND COUSCOUS

*Most, if not all, commercially sold couscous is parcooked
nowadays. It thus cooks very quickly, which makes it a
convenient and unusual alternative to rice. In this recipe the
couscous is served with harissa, a traditional North African hot
chilli sauce. If you wish, you may add cooked chicken pieces at
the same time as the tomatoes.*

1 tablespoon olive oil
1 onion, sliced
8 oz (225g) courgettes, sliced
8 oz (225g) mushrooms,
  sliced
1 red pepper, seeded and
  chopped
2 carrots, thinly sliced
14 oz (400g) can tomatoes
2 oz (50g) raisins
2 oz (50g) flaked almonds
1 teaspoon chilli sauce or
  harissa
8 oz (225g) couscous
1½ pints (825ml) boiling
  water
Parsley to garnish

Serves 4

Heat the oil in a large saucepan, add
the onion and sauté for 2 minutes.
Add the courgettes, mushrooms, red
pepper and carrots and sauté for a
further 2 minutes. Add the
tomatoes, raisins, flaked almonds,
chilli sauce or harissa and enough
water to cover. Simmer until the
vegetables are just tender, about
6–8 minutes. Meanwhile pour the
boiling water over the couscous and
leave to stand for 5 minutes. Serve
the vegetables on a bed of couscous,
garnished with parsley.

PASTA WITH CAULIFLOWER, SARDINE AND ANCHOVY SAUCE

This simple Sicilian dish is best served with a tossed green salad.

1 large cauliflower, separated
   into florets
Salt
3–4 tablespoons olive oil
8 oz (225g) fresh sardines,
   filleted
2 oz (50g) onion, sliced
4 cloves garlic, crushed
½ teaspoon ground cloves
¼ teaspoon ground
   cinnamon
4 oz (100g) tomato purée
2 oz (50g) can anchovies,
   drained
1¼ lb (550g) long macaroni
Freshly ground black pepper
   to taste

Serves 6

Boil the cauliflower florets in salted water for about 5 minutes then drain, reserving the cooking liquid. Heat the oil in a large heavy pan, add the cauliflower, sardine fillets, onion and garlic. Cook over a moderate heat, stirring frequently, for 3 minutes. Add the cloves, cinnamon and tomato purée and stir well. Cover and simmer for 10–15 minutes, adding a tablespoon or two of the cauliflower water if the mixture becomes dry. Add the anchovies and cook for a further 5 minutes. Meanwhile, cook the pasta in boiling water, including the water from cooking the cauliflower, until *al dente*. Drain and stir the pasta into the sauce. Add freshly ground black pepper to taste then serve immediately.

TAGLIATELLE WITH FISH AND TOMATO SAUCE

2 tablespoons olive oil
8 oz (225g) onions, finely chopped
1–2 cloves garlic, chopped
1 green pepper, cut into strips
Freshly ground black pepper to taste
1 tablespoon chopped fresh tarragon, or dried tarragon to taste
2×14 oz (400g) cans chopped tomatoes
1 lb (450g) cod or haddock, skinned and cut into cubes
1 lb (450g) green tagliatelle

Serves 4

Heat the oil in a heavy saucepan, then add the chopped onions, garlic and green pepper strips and fry gently until softened, about 8 minutes. Add black pepper, the tarragon, if using dried, the chopped tomatoes and the fish. Cook, uncovered, for about 10 minutes, until the fish is tender but not falling apart. If using fresh tarragon, stir it in now. Cook the tagliatelle in plenty of boiling salted water until *al dente*. Drain, and mix with the fish and tomato sauce, combining well. Serve at once.

SPAGHETTI WITH TOMATO AND ANCHOVY SAUCE

A real taste of Italy, colourful and full of flavour. Very easy and inexpensive.

3 tablespoons olive oil
1–2 cloves garlic, crushed
2 oz (50g) can anchovy
  fillets
1 oz (25g) fresh parsley,
  chopped
14 oz (400g) can chopped
  tomatoes
Salt and freshly ground
  black pepper to taste
1 lb (450g) wholemeal
  spaghetti

Serves 4

Heat the oil in a small saucepan and cook the garlic gently for 1 minute without browning. Add the anchovy fillets (with their oil) and cook for a further minute. Stir in the tomatoes, add salt and pepper and bring the sauce to a gentle boil. Simmer, uncovered, for about 30 minutes, stirring now and then. Meanwhile, cook the spaghetti in plenty of boiling salted water until *al dente*. Drain, then mix with the sauce and parsley to coat the pasta evenly. Serve at once.

PASTA WITH TOMATO, BASIL AND PINE NUT SAUCE

12 oz (350g) wholewheat
  pasta
4 oz (100g) pine nuts
3 tablespoons chopped fresh
  basil
14 oz (400g) can tomatoes
2 tablespoons olive oil
Salt and freshly ground
  black pepper to taste
Parmesan cheese, grated

Serves 4

Cook the pasta in plenty of boiling salted water until *al dente*. Meanwhile blend all the remaining ingredients in a food processor or blender. Transfer the mixture to a pan and heat gently. Drain the pasta, pour over the sauce, toss together and serve, topped with Parmesan cheese.

PASTA BOWS WITH MUSHROOMS AND OLIVE SAUCE

A rich, brown mushroom sauce with subtle flavouring. Great with a glass of wine and a tossed green salad.

3 tablespoons olive oil
1 lb (450g) mushrooms, left whole if small, sliced if large
1–2 cloves garlic, crushed
1 teaspoon dried marjoram
Salt and freshly ground black pepper to taste
4 fl oz (100ml) white wine
1 oz (25g) plain flour
3 tablespoons tomato purée
8 fl oz (225ml) vegetable stock or water
4 oz (100g) stoned black olives, chopped
1 lb (450g) pasta bows

Serves 4

Heat the olive oil in a saucepan and add the mushrooms; cook for 2 minutes, stirring often. Add the garlic, marjoram and salt and pepper. Leave to cook for 2 minutes, then turn up the heat and pour in the wine. Boil rapidly until the foam subsides, then tip in the flour and stir briskly. Add the tomato purée and the vegetable stock or water. Stir well and then add the olives. Leave to simmer covered for 20 minutes, stirring often. Meanwhile, cook the pasta bows in plenty of boiling, salted water until *al dente*. Drain, mix with the mushroom and olive sauce and serve immediately.

Note Freshly grated Parmesan cheese, handed separately, makes this extra delicious.

HARICOT BEANS WITH MARROW AND SWEETCORN

This is a useful dish for the autumn when marrows are plentiful and cheap. Courgettes may be substituted for the marrow at other times.

3 tablespoons olive oil
4 oz (100g) onion, chopped
1 clove garlic, chopped
14 oz (400g) can chopped
  tomatoes
1 teaspoon paprika
1 teaspoon chilli sauce
14 oz (400g) can haricot
  beans, drained or 6 oz
  (175g) dried haricot beans,
  soaked overnight, cooked
  until tender and drained
1 lb (450g) marrow, coarsely
  diced
4 oz (100g) frozen sweetcorn
  kernels
Salt and freshly ground
  black pepper to taste

Serves 4

Heat the olive oil in a large saucepan, fry the onion in it for about 5 minutes until soft, then add the garlic, tomatoes, paprika and chilli sauce. Cook fairly fast for 10 minutes or so until the mixture reduces and thickens slightly. Stir in the drained beans and the marrow. Simmer for a further 10 minutes until the marrow is nearly cooked. Add the corn kernels and heat through thoroughly. Season to taste and serve.

BUTTERBEAN RISSOLES

A favourite with children, who tend to enjoy the sweetness of the beans.

2×14 oz (400g) cans
    butterbeans, drained or 14
    oz (400g) dried
    butterbeans, soaked
    overnight, cooked until
    tender and drained
8 oz (225g) onions, finely
    chopped
3 oz (75g) butter
3 oz (75g) fresh brown
    breadcrumbs
2 eggs
4 oz (100g) fruit chutney
Juice of ½ lemon
Salt and freshly ground
    black pepper to taste

TO FINISH
Beaten egg (of 1 large egg)
More breadcrumbs, approx.
    2 oz (50g)
Oil for shallow-frying

Serves 4

Mash the drained butterbeans or purée them in a blender. Fry the onions in the butter until softened but not brown then remove from the heat. Add the butterbeans, breadcrumbs, eggs, chutney and lemon juice to the onion. Season well and stir until thoroughly combined. Shape into rissoles and dip into the beaten egg then into the breadcrumbs. Shallow-fry in hot oil then drain well on paper towels. Serve with green salad and tomato ketchup.

SPINACH AND CHICKPEA CURRY

3 tablespoons vegetable oil
8 oz (225g) onions, chopped
4 cloves garlic, crushed
1 teaspoon cumin seeds
1 teaspoon chilli powder
1 teaspoon dried ginger
6 cardamom pods
8 oz (225g) frozen spinach, drained and chopped or 1 lb (450g) fresh spinach, washed
2×14 oz (400g) cans chickpeas, drained or 14 oz (400g) dried chickpeas, soaked overnight, cooked until tender and drained
14 oz (400g) tomatoes, chopped
2 tablespoons tomato purée
Salt to taste

Serves 4

Heat the oil in a large pan, add the onions and garlic and fry until softened. Add the spices and cook for a further 2 minutes. Add the spinach, stirring vigorously. Next, add the chickpeas, tomatoes and tomato purée. Season with salt. Add a little water if the curry seems dry. Simmer covered for about 20 minutes then serve.

BEAN PLAKI

In this Greek dish, beans are cooked with vegetables, including tomatoes, then chilled and dressed with oil and vinegar. It's also good served hot, with garlic bread. The ingredients vary slightly according to whether you want to serve the dish hot or cold (see method).

4 fl oz (100ml) olive oil
2 cloves garlic, crushed
2 onions, finely sliced
1 carrot, diced
2 stalks celery with leaves, chopped
3 tablespoons chopped fresh parsley
1 bay leaf, crumbled
1 teaspoon dried oregano
6 tomatoes, peeled and chopped, or 1 lb (450g) canned tomatoes
2×14 oz (400g) cans haricot beans or 14 oz (400g) dried haricot beans, soaked overnight, cooked until tender and drained
Salt to taste

TO SERVE COLD
2 tablespoons wine vinegar
2 tablespoons olive oil or vegetable oil
Olives for garnish

Serves 6

Heat the olive oil in a heavy saucepan, then add the garlic, onions, carrot and celery and sauté until softened but not browned. Stir in 2 tablespoons of the parsley, the bay leaf, oregano and tomatoes. Simmer covered for 15 minutes or until thoroughly blended. Add the beans, their liquid and 4 fl oz (100ml) water and bring to the boil. Cover, reduce the heat and simmer for 30 minutes. After 15 minutes check the pan and leave the lid off if the mixture is too liquid or add water if it is too dry. The consistency should be quite thick. Add salt to taste and serve hot, garnished with the remaining parsley.

Alternatively, to serve cold, allow the mixture to cool, then stir in the vinegar and oil. Garnish with olives and the remaining parsley.

KIDNEY BEANS AND RICE IN TOMATO SAUCE

1 tablespoon olive oil
1 small onion, finely
  chopped
1 pint (550ml) tomato juice
14 oz (400g) can red kidney
  beans or 6 oz (175g) dried
  kidney beans, soaked
  overnight, cooked until
  tender and drained
  (reserve the liquid)
8 oz (225g) long grain rice
Salt and freshly ground
  black pepper to taste
½–1 teaspoon chilli sauce
  (optional)
Freshly grated Parmesan
  cheese to garnish

Serves 4–6

Heat the olive oil in a fairly large pan and sauté the onion in it until softened. Make up the tomato juice to 1½ pints (825ml) with the liquid from the kidney beans. Add this to the pan with the rice, beans, salt and black pepper and chilli sauce, if using. Bring to the boil, reduce the heat, cover and simmer until the rice is tender, about 20 minutes. Add more liquid if the rice is in danger of drying out. Serve sprinkled with Parmesan cheese.

BUTTERBEAN AND TOMATO PIE WITH TWO-CHEESE TOPPING

2×14 oz (400g) cans
 butterbeans or 14 oz
 (400g) dried butterbeans,
 soaked overnight, cooked
 until tender and drained
12 oz (350g) onions,
 chopped
2 green peppers, chopped
2 tablespoons olive oil
14 oz (400g) can chopped
 tomatoes
1 tablespoon tomato purée
1 tablespoon brown sugar
1 teaspoon dried oregano
Salt and freshly ground
 black pepper

TOPPING
4 oz (100g) cheese, grated
8 oz (225g) cottage cheese
1 egg, beaten

Serves 4

Preheat the oven to 375°F (190°C, gas mark 5). Rinse and drain the beans. Fry the onions and green peppers in the olive oil for 2–3 minutes. Add the chopped tomatoes, tomato purée, brown sugar and oregano and season well. Simmer for 5 minutes, then add the beans. Transfer the mixture to a casserole dish. If necessary, add a little water and stir it in so that the beans are covered with liquid. Mix the topping ingredients together and spread over the bean mixture. Bake in the preheated oven for 25 minutes until golden brown and bubbly.

JACK'S BEANCURD WITH PINEAPPLE

This delicious sweet and sour stir-fry dish was created by Jack Angelo. Serve with boiled rice.

12 oz (350g) beancurd (tofu)
14 oz (400g) can pineapple
chunks in syrup
1 teaspoon cornflour
2 tablespoons soya sauce
2 tablespoons dry sherry or
rice wine
4 tablespoons vegetable oil
1 spring onion, chopped
4 oz (100g) beansprouts

Serves 4

Drain the beancurd and cut it into small cubes. Drain the syrup from the pineapple and reserve 1 tablespoon. Dissolve the cornflour in this in a small bowl and stir in the soya sauce and sherry or rice wine. Stir in the beancurd and leave to stand for 15 minutes. Heat 2 tablespoons of the oil in a wok or large frying pan and stir-fry the beancurd, with its marinade until most of the liquid is absorbed. Remove the beancurd from the pan and drain. Add the remaining oil to the pan and stir-fry the spring onion, beansprouts and pineapple chunks for 1 minute. Return the beancurd to the pan and cook together for 2 minutes.

FRIED TOFU WITH DIPPING SAUCES

2×6 oz (175g) squares of
  tofu, cut into 3 in (7.5cm)
  squares
Cornflour
Oil for deep frying

DIPPING SAUCE 1
2 tablespoons shery
3 tablespoons dark soya
  sauce
1 tablespoon sugar

DIPPING SAUCE 2
3 tablespoons dark soya
  sauce
1 tablespoon prepared
  mustard
1 teaspoon dark brown
  sugar
1 teaspoon rice vinegar or
  cider vinegar
1 teaspoon minced spring
  onion

Serves 4

Coat the pieces of tofu in cornflour,
taking care not to break them. Then
deep-fry them over a moderate heat
for 4 minutes until light golden in
colour. Lift the tofu out carefully
and drain. Combine the ingredients
for one or both of the dipping
sauces and serve with the hot tofu.

VEGETABLES

MIXED VEGETABLE BHAJI

Any vegetables in season may be used in this spicy hot bhaji dish and the selection given below is only a suggestion. It is a convenient way of using up odds and ends of vegetables.

4 oz (100g) ghee or butter
½ onion, chopped
4 cloves garlic, crushed
1 teaspoon cumin seeds
1 teaspoon turmeric
2 carrots, sliced
½ small cabbage, coarsely
  chopped
4 oz (100g) young okra pods
  or runner beans (cut
  runner beans in half)
Salt to taste
2 large tomatoes, sliced
1–2 fresh green chillies,
  finely chopped
1 in (2.5cm) piece ginger
  root, peeled and grated
1 tablespoon finely chopped
  fresh coriander leaves

Serves 4

Heat the ghee or butter in a large heavy saucepan and sauté the onion until golden brown. Add the garlic, cumin seeds and turmeric, stir and cook for a minute or two. Add the carrots, cabbage, okra or runner beans and cook, stirring, over a low to moderate heat for 5 minutes. Add salt to taste then cover the pan and simmer over a very low heat for 10 minutes. Stir in the tomatoes, chillies and ginger, cover the pan again and simmer for a further 10–15 minutes or until all the vegetables are tender. If the contents of the pan are too liquid, cook uncovered for the last period of the cooking time. Serve garnished with the coriander leaves.

CHESTNUT AND VEGETABLE CASSEROLE

Vacuum-packed cooked chestnuts are now available in many specialist food shops. They are most convenient to use, and are good in both sweet and savoury dishes. If you wish to use fresh chestnuts in this recipe, slash the skins, parboil them for 5 minutes, then peel off both the outer skin and the fine inner skin.

3 oz (75g) butter
1 onion, diced
1 green pepper, seeded and sliced
4 oz (100g) mushrooms, sliced
1 lb (450g) cooked chestnuts (see above)
1 egg, beaten
2 tablespoons chopped fresh parsley
Salt and freshly ground black pepper to taste
2 oz (50g) fresh breadcrumbs

Serves 4

Preheat the oven to 375°F (190°C, gas mark 5). Melt half the butter in a heavy saucepan and sauté the onion and green pepper until soft. Add the mushrooms and sauté for a further 2 minutes then remove from the heat. Chop the chestnuts in half and combine with the vegetables. Add the beaten egg, parsley and salt and black pepper and mix well. Pour the mixture into a greased casserole dish and sprinkle the breadcrumbs over the top. Dot with the remaining butter and bake in the preheated oven for 30 minutes or until well browned.

VARIATION
Substitute 8 oz (225g) chopped nuts for the chestnuts.

KYOTO CUCUMBER AND MUSHROOMS

A Japanese dish in which cucumber is cooked with mushrooms in a sweet soya sauce.

1 cucumber, sliced
Salt
2 tablespoons vegetable oil
8 oz (225g) mushrooms, sliced
3 tablespoons soya sauce
2 teaspoons sugar
2 tablespoons sesame seeds, dry-roasted

Serves 4 as a side dish

Layer the cucumber slices in a colander, adding salt to each layer. Leave to stand for 30 minutes, then rinse, drain and pat dry. Heat the oil in a heavy pan, add the mushrooms and cucumber and cook over a high heat, stirring occasionally, until the vegetables are tender, 2–3 minutes. Remove from the heat. Stir in the soya sauce and sugar and serve sprinkled with the sesame seeds.

MUSHROOM AND COCONUT CURRY

2 dried red chillies, crushed
1 teaspoon ground cumin
1 teaspoon ground coriander
½ teaspoon chilli sauce or
  Tabasco
4 cloves garlic, crushed
Salt
8 oz (225g) onions, finely
  chopped
2 tablespoons vegetable oil
1½ lbs (675g) small button
  mushrooms
½ pint (275ml) hot
  vegetable stock
4 oz (100g) creamed coconut
  (in block form)

Serves 4

Blend the chillies, spices, chilli sauce or Tabasco, garlic and a little salt to a paste with the back of a knife blade. Gently fry the onions and the blended spice mixture in the oil for 5 minutes, or until the onions begin to soften. Add the mushrooms and fry gently, stirring to mix in the spices thoroughly, for a further 10 minutes. Dissolve the creamed coconut in the hot vegetable stock. Add to the mushrooms and simmer for another 10–15 minutes until the sauce thickens. Serve with rice or naan bread and perhaps spiced spinach.

LENTIL AND WINTER VEGETABLE CASSEROLE

3 tablespoons vegetable oil
1½ lbs (675g) mixed root
  vegetables, such as
  parsnip, carrot and turnip,
  peeled and diced
2 large onions, chopped
4 stalks celery, sliced
14 oz (400g) can continental
  lentils/6 oz (175g) dried
  lentils, soaked for 4 hours
  and drained
2 cloves garlic, crushed
14 oz (400g) can tomatoes
½ pint (275ml) vegetable
  stock
Salt and freshly ground
  black pepper to taste
¼ pint (150ml) plain yogurt

Serves 4

Heat the oil in a large saucepan, then add the root vegetables, onions and celery. Fry for about 5 minutes without browning the vegetables. Add the lentils, garlic, tomatoes and stock (reserve 2 fl oz/50ml), stir and cook for a further 5 minutes. Cover and simmer for 15 minutes (30 minutes if using dried lentils). If the mixture becomes too dry, add the reserved vegetable stock (and if needed just enough extra water to cover). Season to taste and cook for a further 5 minutes. Serve in individual bowls with a dollop of yogurt.

FENNEL WITH GINGER

This is an old English country recipe in which the fennel is served over thick slices of brown bread.

1½ lbs (675g) fennel bulbs, trimmed, cleaned and cut into matchsticks
8 oz (225g) onions, thickly sliced
1 heaped teaspoon ground ginger
1 level teaspoon powdered saffron
½ teaspoon salt
2 tablespoons olive oil or other good-quality oil
¼ pt (150ml) each dry white wine and water
6 thick slices coarse wholemeal bread

Serves 6

Put the fennel in a wide pan with the onions. Sprinkle over the spices and salt, then the oil, and finally pour over the wine and water. Bring to the boil, cover and simmer for 20–30 minutes or until the fennel is cooked without being mushy. Stir once or twice during cooking to make sure the spices are well distributed. To serve, place a slice of bread on each warmed plate, cover it with the fennel and pour over the juices.

BAKED CAULIFLOWER WITH NUTS AND CHEESE

A nutritious dish and an interesting variation on the usual cauliflower cheese recipe.

2 cauliflowers, broken into small florets
2 oz (50g) butter
2 oz (50g) plain flour
1 pint (550ml) milk
4 oz (100g) salted peanuts
7 oz (200g) Cheddar cheese, grated
Pinch of ground nutmeg (optional)
Salt and freshly ground black pepper to taste

Serves 4

Preheat the oven to 425°F (220°C, gas mark 7). Steam the cauliflower florets over boiling water, until they are cooked but still crunchy, about 8 minutes. Melt the butter in a pan, stir in the flour and cook for a minute or two. Stir in the milk then simmer for 10 minutes until thick. If the sauce is too thick, add a little of the cooking liquid from the cauliflower. In a greased deep casserole dish make layers of the cauliflower florets, sauce, peanuts and cheese. Sprinkle each layer with nutmeg, if using, and salt and pepper. Finish with a layer of cheese. Bake in the preheated oven for 15 minutes until brown and bubbly.

STIR-FRIED SWEET AND SOUR VEGETABLES

Stir-fried vegetables are only lightly cooked and should retain some crunch. This dish can also be served cold as a salad. Add more soya sauce than suggested, if you prefer. Add 2 teaspoons chopped fresh ginger root with the garlic and onion if you like ginger.

3 tablespoons vegetable oil
2 cloves garlic, crushed
1 onion, finely chopped
1 carrot, finely sliced
2 red or green peppers, seeded and cut into strips
8 oz (225g) white cabbage, finely shredded
6 radishes, sliced
6 oz (175g) beansprouts, washed and drained
2 tablespoons wine vinegar
2 tablespoons clear honey
2 tablespoons tamari or other soya sauce

Serves 4

Heat the oil in a wok or a large frying pan and add the garlic, onion, carrot and peppers. Stir-fry over a medium heat for 3–4 minutes. Add the cabbage and stir-fry for another 3 minutes, then add the radishes and beansprouts and stir-fry for a further minute. In a bowl mix together the vinegar, honey and soya sauce. Pour the mixture over the vegetables, stir briefly and serve immediately.

SAUTÉED POTATOES WITH HAZELNUT SAUCE

This recipe uses hazelnut oil. It is an expensive ingredient for one dish but if kept in the store cupboard it can be used to prepare delicious, nutty-flavoured salad dressings.

1 lb (450g) new potatoes
½ oz (15g) hazelnuts
Hazelnut oil
3 fl oz (75ml) crème fraîche
  or thick cream
Squeeze of lemon juice
Salt and freshly ground
  black pepper to taste
Small bunch of fresh chives,
  chopped (optional)

Serves 4

Boil the potatoes in their skins. Meanwhile simmer the hazelnuts in a little water for 3–4 minutes then drain, peel off the skins and dry. Gently fry the hazelnuts in a little hazelnut oil until brown. Set aside to cool then crush roughly. Once the potatoes are cooked, drain and peel them then sauté, either whole or sliced, in 1–2 tablespoons hazelnut oil. Once they are crispy and golden, transfer them to a hot serving dish while you prepare the sauce. Do not prepare them in advance or they will go soggy. Wipe out the pan, add 1–2 tablespoons more hazelnut oil, then add the crème fraîche or thick cream. Heat gently, stirring briskly until the mixture combines and thickens. Once it has reduced to a coating sauce add a squeeze of lemon juice and salt and black pepper. Pour the sauce over the potatoes and scatter over the crushed hazelnuts and the chopped chives, if using. Serve at once.

POTATOES IN HOT GARLIC SAUCE

1 lb (450g) potatoes, peeled and finely chopped
3 tablespoons vegetable oil
4 cloves garlic, finely chopped
1 fresh green chilli, seeded and sliced
Pinch of chilli powder
Pinch of freshly ground black pepper
4 fl oz (100ml) stock or water

Serves 4

Cook the potatoes in boiling salted water until almost tender, then drain. Heat the oil in a wok or large frying pan and fry the garlic and fresh chilli for 1 minute. Stir in the chilli powder and black pepper. Add the potatoes and fry until they begin to brown. Add the stock or water and cook for a further 3–5 minutes then serve.

CHILLI-HOT MIXED VEGETABLES IN COCONUT AND YOGURT

The coconut and yogurt soothe the fiery taste of the chillies in this Indonesian-style dish.

1½ lb (675g) mixed vegetables, prepared and cut into bite-sized pieces, e.g. carrots, courgettes, green beans, peppers, cauliflower, peas, Chinese cabbage, water chestnuts etc.
3 oz (75g) desiccated coconut
2 cloves garlic, crushed
2–3 fresh green chillies, seeded, chopped
1 teaspoon cumin seeds
1 teaspoon salt
1 teaspoon curry paste
½ lime, sliced
¼ pint (150g) plain yogurt

Serves 4

Bring 6 fl oz (175ml) water to the boil in a heavy saucepan then add the vegetables in order of cooking times and simmer until they are half cooked. Meanwhile, mix the coconut, garlic, chillies, cumin seeds and salt together. Reduce the heat under the vegetables and add the coconut and spice mixture, the curry paste and the lime slices. Stir and simmer for 10 minutes. Stir in the yogurt and serve.

HUNAN VEGETABLE HOTPOT

You will need a largish cooking pot for this very simple hotpot. If the pot is nice enough, bring it to the table and serve the meal from it in large soup plates. The dish needs livening up for some tastes, so serve with a small dish of chilli sauce and black or white pepper in a pepper mill.

2 pints (1.1 litres) vegetable stock
4 oz (100g) cauliflower florets
2 courgettes, diagonally sliced
2 red or yellow peppers, seeded and quartered
3 oz (75g) spring onions, chopped
4 oz (100g) mangetout
4 oz (100g) mushrooms, sliced
2 small carrots, sliced
2 small turnips, peeled and sliced
2 in (5cm) piece ginger root, peeled and grated
Soya sauce to taste

Serves 4

Bring the stock to the boil in a large pot. Add the vegetables, ginger and soya sauce, then cook slowly (covered) until all the vegetables are tender, about 30 minutes.

COUNTRY CASSEROLE

A big-hearted casserole, warm and sustaining on a cold day.

4 small onions, thinly sliced
Vegetable oil for shallow-
    frying
12 oz (350g) mushrooms,
    sliced
2×14 oz (400g) cans
    butterbeans
6 tomatoes, roughly chopped
Salt and freshly ground
    black pepper to taste
4 oz (100g) fresh brown
    breadcrumbs
4 oz (100g) cheese, grated

Serves 4

Sauté the onions in the oil until transparent. Add the sliced mushrooms and continue frying for 5–6 minutes. Drain the butterbeans, add them with the chopped tomatoes to the onions and mushrooms. Season with salt and black pepper and heat through. Place in an ovenproof dish and sprinkle with the breadcrumbs and grated cheese. Brown under a hot grill and serve at once.

TWO-BEAN AND VEGETABLE HOTPOT

The convenience of canned beans makes this dish quick and easy to prepare. Try it with other beans, such as chickpeas, as well as these recommended in the recipe.

14 oz (400g) can borlotti beans
14 oz (400g) can butterbeans
4 oz (100g) fresh or frozen green beans, chopped
14 oz (400g) can chopped tomatoes
1 lb (450g) potatoes, peeled and coarsely grated
1 tablespoon tomato purée
1 teaspoon dried mixed herbs
Salt and freshly ground black pepper to taste
4 oz (100g) cheese, grated

Serves 4

Preheat the oven to 400°F (200°C, gas mark 6). Mix the borlotti and butterbeans with the green beans, tomatoes, potatoes, tomato purée, herbs and seasoning then transfer to an ovenproof casserole dish. Cover and cook in the preheated oven for about 35 minutes or until the potatoes are tender. Serve in bowls and top with the grated cheese.

STIR-FRIED CHICKEN AND ASPARAGUS

This is not the best way to use expensive, good-quality asparagus but it is suitable for the cheaper, thin stalks of sprue. It's also an unusual and simple way of using up leftover cooked chicken.

2 tablespoons sesame oil or vegetable oil
1 in (2.5cm) piece fresh ginger root, peeled and finely chopped
1 clove garlic, crushed
10 oz (275g) asparagus, trimmed and cut into 1 in (2.5cm) lengths
2 cooked chicken breasts or other chicken meat, cut into bite-sized pieces
4 tablespoons chicken stock or water
1 tablespoon rice wine or dry sherry
2 teaspoons cornflour

Serves 2–3

Heat half the oil in a wok or large frying pan. Stir-fry the ginger and garlic for less than a minute and then toss in the asparagus. Stir-fry for 1 minute. Remove the asparagus with a slotted spoon and set aside. Add the remaining oil and the chicken to the pan and stir until thoroughly heated through. Remove from the heat and add the stock or water and rice wine or sherry (be careful in case the oil spits). Stir well and sprinkle in the cornflour. Return to the heat and mix well. Return the asparagus to the pan, toss gently to heat through and serve immediately.

Note: Cooked chicken should only be reheated if it was cooked within the previous 48 hours and then stored in a refrigerator.

VEGETABLE BIRIANI

This is very easy to make, but it is also a versatile recipe and you can use whichever combination of vegetables you have at hand. Serve with chutney and poppadums.

4 oz (100g) onion, chopped
1 clove garlic, crushed
1 tablespoon vegetable oil
2 teaspoons ground turmeric
2 teaspoons ground coriander
4 cardamom pods (optional)
6 oz (175g) green or brown lentils, soaked for 4 hours
8 oz (225g) carrots, peeled and sliced
4 oz (100g) button mushrooms
1 pint (550ml) vegetable stock
8 oz (225g) brown rice
4 oz (100g) frozen peas
4 oz (100g) fresh or frozen French beans
2 tomatoes, sliced

Serves 4

Gently sauté the onion and garlic in the oil for 7 minutes. Add the spices and cook for a further 2 minutes. Add the lentils, carrots, mushrooms, stock and rice. Bring to the boil, cover and simmer for 30 minutes or until lentils and rice are tender. After 25 minutes before the rice is ready, add the peas and French beans. Serve garnished with the tomato slices.

MACKEREL GRILLED WITH MUSTARD

This simple dish depends on good ingredients for its success, so choose very fresh fish and a good, mild, wholegrain mustard. Serve with brown bread and salad.

2 fresh mackerel, about 10 oz (275g) each, cleaned and heads removed
2 tablespoons mild wholegrain mustard
1 tablespoon vegetable oil
Lemon wedges
Freshly milled black pepper

Serves 2

Preheat the grill to medium. Cut three fairly deep slashes in each side of the fish then brush each side with the mustard. Brush a baking sheet with some of the oil or cover the grill pan with kitchen foil and brush with oil. Brush both sides of each fish with the remaining oil and grill for 5 minutes on each side or until tender but not overcooked. Serve with lemon wedges and black pepper in a mill.

PEPPERED COD

Serve this tasty and very quick dish with fresh green vegetables.

1 teaspoon green
  peppercorns
1 teaspoon capers
2 oz (50g) butter
2 teaspoons lemon juice
2×6 oz (175g) cod fillets,
  skinned
A little vegetable oil
Paprika, to taste

Serves 2

Preheat the grill to hot. With a small, sharp knife chop the peppercorns and capers as finely as you can. Combine them with the butter and lemon juice and spread the mixture over the top of the cod fillets. Line the grill pan with kitchen foil, brush with a little oil and lay the fillets on it, coated side up. Grill for 5 minutes (one side only) and serve, sprinkled with paprika to taste.

STEAMED WHITING, CHINESE STYLE

This way of cooking fish seals in all the juices and keeps it moist. Serve with boiled rice and mangetout.

8 whiting fillets, about 4 oz (100g) each
2 green peppers, seeded
Juice of 1 lemon
2 tablespoons soya sauce
½ oz (15g) fresh ginger root, peeled and cut into fine strips

SAUCE
4 tablespoons soya sauce
2 teaspoons tomato purée
2 tablespoons sunflower oil

Serves 4

Cut the whiting fillets lengthwise in half to make 16 long strips. Cut each pepper into 8 strips. Mix the lemon juice and soya sauce together. Brush some of this mixture over the fish and reserve the rest. Sprinkle the fish with the fresh ginger. Put a piece of pepper on the tail end of each fish strip and roll up neatly. Divide the whiting rolls between four 10 in (25cm) square pieces of oiled foil and fold into loose packets. Put into a large colander and cover with more foil. Bring a large pan of water to the boil. Put the colander over the pan and steam the fish for 15 minutes. Meanwhile, mix the reserved soya sauce and lemon juice mixture with the sauce ingredients. Pour into a small saucepan and simmer to heat through without boiling. Put the fish parcels on warm plates and pass the sauce separately.

FISH CASSEROLE

A hearty dish of white fish and vegetables.

1 tablespoon olive oil
4 oz (100g) onion, thinly
  sliced
14 oz (400g) can chopped
  tomatoes
1 lb (450g) potatoes, diced
Salt and freshly ground
  black pepper to taste
1 lb (450g) any firm white
  fish, cut into large chunks
Juice of 1 lemon
2 teaspoons tomato purée
4 tablespoons dry white
  wine
6 oz (175g) courgettes,
  thickly sliced
4 oz (100g) fresh French
  beans
4 oz (100g) fresh or frozen
  broad beans
1 oz (25g) fresh parsley,
  chopped

Serves 4

Heat the oil in a large saucepan, add the onion and fry until softened. Add the tomatoes and diced potatoes. Cover and simmer for 15 minutes, until the potatoes are just tender. Meanwhile, season the fish and sprinkle with the lemon juice. Mix the tomato purée with the white wine and stir into the saucepan. Add the fish chunks, courgettes, french beans and broad beans to the pan and stir gently to mix everything together. Simmer for 10 minutes until the fish is tender. Sprinkle with the parsley and serve hot in large bowls.

CHIORRO

This is a Basque fish dish. It's great if you love garlic.

3 tablespoons olive oil
1 lb (450g) onions, thinly
  sliced
12 cloves garlic, finely
  chopped
1 tablespoon tomato purée
2 teaspoons paprika
Pinch of cayenne pepper
Pinch of ground mace
Salt and freshly ground
  black pepper to taste
½ pint (275ml) red wine
¼ pint (150ml) water
1½ lbs (675g) fresh or
  frozen cod steaks
1 tablespoon lemon juice

Serves 4

Preheat the oven to 350°F (180°C, gas mark 4). Heat the olive oil in a shallow saucepan, add the onions and garlic, cover the pan and cook slowly until softened. Then remove the lid and increase the heat to brown them lightly. Add the tomato purée, spices and salt and pepper, stir well, then add the wine and the water. Bring to the boil and simmer, with the lid off, for 10–15 minutes. Remove from the heat and adjust the seasoning.

Lay the fish steaks in a greased ovenproof dish, sprinkle with the lemon juice, cover and poach them in the preheated oven for 15–20 minutes. When cooked, remove from the oven and transfer to warmed serving plates. Quickly reheat the sauce, if necessary. Pour a good spoonful of the sauce over each piece of fish. Serve very hot, with plenty of crusty bread to dip in the sauce.

GRILLED MACKEREL WITH APPLE PURÉE

With its oily flesh, mackerel is best simply grilled and accompanied with a sharply flavoured sauce such as this one. Serve with boiled new potatoes and broccoli.

2 cooking apples, peeled, cored and sliced
4 tablespoons dry cider
4 small mackerel, gutted, rinsed and dried
½ oz (15g) fresh parsley, chopped
4 lemon slices

Serves 4

Put the apples in a saucepan with the cider, cover and cook gently until soft. Beat with a wooden spoon until a smooth purée is obtained. Set aside and keep warm.

Preheat the grill to hot. With a sharp knife, make 2 or 3 diagonal slashes on each side of the mackerel. Cook them under the hot grill on oiled foil for about 5 minutes each side. Put the mackerel on a warmed serving dish, garnished with the parsley and lemon slices. Serve the apple purée separately.

BAKED COD IN TOMATO SAUCE

*This is a straightforward standard recipe but its simplicity is its
strength and it works well. To ring the changes add a pinch of
freshly ground coriander to the tomato sauce and use fresh
coriander leaves in place of the parsley.*

4 tablespoons olive oil
1 clove garlic, crushed
14 oz (400g) can chopped
   tomatoes
4 tablespoons white wine
Salt and freshly ground
   black pepper to taste
4 fresh or frozen cod steaks
½ oz (15g) fresh parsley,
   chopped

Serves 4

Preheat the oven to 375°F (190°C,
gas mark 5). Heat the oil in a
saucepan, add the garlic, tomatoes,
wine and salt and pepper. Simmer
for 7–10 minutes, stirring
occasionally. Pour half the sauce into
a shallow casserole dish, lay the cod
steaks on top and cover with the rest
of the sauce. Cover and bake in the
preheated oven for about 20 minutes
until the fish is cooked through.
Sprinkle with the chopped parsley
and serve with new potatoes.

GRILLED FISH WITH LEMON SAUCE AND PARMESAN

Serve with potatoes or pasta.

4 firm white fish fillets,
   lightly brushed with a
   little oil
1 oz (25g) butter
1 oz (25g) plain flour
½ pint (275ml) milk
Salt and freshly ground
   black pepper to taste
Grated rind and juice of ½
   lemon
2 tablespoons chopped fresh
   chives
1½ oz (40g) Parmesan
   cheese, freshly grated

Serves 4

Preheat the grill to hot. Put the fish fillets in a well greased cast-iron gratin dish and grill, turning once, for about 5–8 minutes, until the fish flakes when pierced with the tip of a knife. Meanwhile, melt the butter in a saucepan, stir in the flour, and cook for 1 minute. Stir in the milk and bring to the boil, stirring constantly. Simmer for 2–3 minutes. Season to taste and stir in the lemon rind and juice and the chives. Drain any juices from the cooked fish into the lemon sauce. Pour the sauce over the fillets and sprinkle on the cheese. Cook under the grill until the cheese browns and the sauce bubbles.

SEVICHE

This spicy Mexican fish dish needs to be started one day in advance, but it is very quick to prepare. The fish is 'cooked' by the action of the lime juice. Serve with fresh crusty bread and a well-dressed green salad.

1 lb (450g) very fresh firm white fish fillets, e.g. cod, sole, monkfish or turbot, skinned and cut into thin strips
4 fl oz (100ml) fresh lime juice
1 small onion, finely chopped
1 large tomato, chopped
1–2 fresh green chillies, seeded and finely chopped
3 tablespoons olive oil
Salt to taste

Serves 4

Put the fish in a glass serving bowl, pour over the lime juice then cover and leave to marinate in the refrigerator for a minimum of 12 hours. Just before serving, stir in the remaining ingredients.

MARINATED SALMON AND MONKFISH

In this Seviche-style dish, raw fish is cooked by the acid in the marinade of citrus juices and vinegar. The preparation time is short but the fish needs to marinate for more than 12 hours before it is ready to eat.

12 oz (350g) salmon, boned and skinned, thinly sliced
12 oz (350g) monkfish, boned and skinned, thinly sliced
1 tablespoon salt
1 tablespoon sugar
Juice and zest of 1 lemon
Juice and zest of 2 oranges
3 tablespoons white wine vinegar
1 fresh green chilli, sliced (optional)
Slices of orange and lemon for garnish

Serves 4

Arrange the sliced fish in one or two layers in a large shallow dish or platter. Combine the salt, sugar, lemon and orange juice and zest and the vinegar and stir to dissolve the salt and sugar, or, if necessary, heat gently then leave to cool. Pour the marinade over the fish, cover with foil and leave to marinate in the refrigerator for 12–24 hours. Serve the fish drained of the marinade but garnished with a little of the lemon and orange zest, the chilli slices, if using, and the fresh lemon and orange slices.

POACHED BRILL WITH CUCUMBER IN WHITE SAUCE

Brill, a yellowy-brown flat fish was once considered the poor cousin of turbot but it has a subtle taste and delicate texture which can be enjoyed in their own right. It is well suited to steaming and poaching. Here, it is served with cooked cucumber, which doesn't overpower the taste of the fish.

4 skinned brill fillets, about 1½ lbs (675g)
Rind and juice of ½ lemon
¼ pint (150ml) water
Salt and freshly ground black pepper to taste
1 large cucumber, peeled and cut into 1 in (2.5cm) cubes
½ oz (15g) butter
½ oz (15g) fresh dill, mint or parsley, chopped
2 oz (50g) Cheddar cheese, grated

SAUCE
1 oz (25g) butter
½ oz (15g) plain flour
¼ pint (150ml) milk

Serves 4

Preheat the oven to 350°F (180°C, gas mark 4). Wash and dry the fish fillets. Place them in a buttered ovenproof dish, tucking the ends of each fillet under. Pour over the lemon juice and water then sprinkle over a little grated lemon rind. Season with salt and pepper, cover with greaseproof paper and cook in the preheated oven for about 15–20 minutes until cooked through. Remove the brill from the oven and keep warm. Drain off and reserve the liquor that it was cooked in.

While the fish is cooking, boil the cucumber cubes in salted water for 1 minute then drain. Melt the butter in a pan, add the cucumber, season to taste and cook gently until almost tender, about 5 minutes. Add the chopped herbs of your choice, then set aside and keep warm.

To make the sauce, melt the butter in a saucepan then stir in the flour and the reserved fish liquor. Stir over a gentle heat until thickened, then add the milk. Bring to the boil and cook rapidly over high heat until the sauce is the consistency of single cream. Pour the sauce over the fish, sprinkle with the grated cheese and brown lightly under a hot grill. Garnish with the cooked cucumber cubes and serve at once.

IKAN GORENG

Ikan Goreng is an Indonesian dish of fish briefly marinated in lime juice then fried in peanut oil. It is particularly good with oily fish, but white fish can be used as well. Serve with boiled rice.

Juice of 2 limes made up to
   8 fl oz (225ml) with water
2 fl oz (50ml) white wine
   vinegar
1 teaspoon salt
6 black peppercorns
2 lb (900g) mackerel, filleted
   (or other fish, oily or
   white)
1 teaspoon turmeric
4 tablespoons peanut oil (or
   other vegetable oil)
Lemon wedges to garnish
Tomato slices to garnish

Serves 4

Mix the diluted lime juice, white wine vinegar, half the salt and peppercorns together, pour over the fish and leave to marinate for 30 minutes, basting occasionally. Remove the fish from the marinade and pat dry with paper towels. Strain the marinade and reserve. Rub the fish all over with the remaining salt and the turmeric. Heat the oil in a large frying pan, add the fish and fry for 4–5 minutes on each side or until the flesh flakes when pierced with a fork. Meanwhile, heat the reserved marinade. Serve the fish with the reserved marinade poured over to taste, garnished with lemon wedges and tomato slices.

TENALI BAKED FISH

A tasty but simple Indian dish which may be grilled or barbecued. Serve with boiled rice mixed with cooked green peas, and sweet lime chutney.

4 thick cod or haddock
  steaks
2 teaspoons salt
2 tablespoons lemon juice
1 teaspoon cayenne pepper
2 garlic cloves, crushed
1 in (2.5cm) piece fresh
  ginger root, peeled and
  grated or finely chopped
2 teaspoons ground
  coriander
4 tablespoons plain yogurt

Serves 4

Dry the fish with paper towels. Mix together the salt, lemon juice and cayenne pepper. Rub this mixture into the fish steaks and set aside for 30 minutes. In a small bowl, mix together the remaining ingredients and spoon over the fish, turning so that the fish steaks are well coated. Set aside again for 1 hour. Grill the fish under a medium-hot grill for 10 minutes on each side until the fish flakes easily when pierced with a fork. Serve immediately with the juices from the grill pan.

GRILLED SALMON WITH BASIL AND LEMON BUTTER

This recipe uses salmon but other fish steaks such as cod or monkfish could be substituted.

2 oz (50g) butter, softened
1 tablespoon finely chopped
 fresh basil
Juice of 1 lemon
Salt and freshly ground
 black pepper to taste
4×5 oz (150g) salmon steaks
A little vegetable oil
Lemon wedges and basil
 sprigs for garnish

Serves 4

Mix together the butter, basil and lemon juice, then add salt and black pepper to taste. Set aside in the refrigerator. Preheat the grill to medium. Brush the salmon steaks with a little vegetable oil, then grill for about 6 minutes on each side or until tender. Remove from under the grill and place a knob of basil and lemon butter on top of each fish steak. Return to the heat until the butter just melts. Serve at once.

GRILLED SALMON WITH STIR-FRIED VEGETABLES

At its very best this dish needs advance planning. However, if you forget or wish to make it immediately, leave out the marinating stage and simply brush the salmon steaks with half the oil and half the soya sauce before grilling.

4×5 oz (150g) salmon steaks, skinned
2 tablespoons walnut, hazelnut or sesame oil
2 teaspoons light soya sauce
6 oz (175g) leeks, trimmed and sliced
4 oz (100g) broccoli florets
2 stalks celery, thinly sliced
4 oz (100g) young spinach leaves
1 oz (25g) blanched almonds

Serves 4

Place the salmon steaks in a dish in a single layer and pour over half the oil and half the soya sauce. Cover and leave to marinate for up to 24 hours in a cool place, turning the fish steaks occasionally.

Bring a saucepan of salted water to the boil. Add the leeks, broccoli, celery and spinach, then as soon as the water returns to the boil, remove the vegetables and drain thoroughly. Preheat the grill to medium then grill the salmon for 3–4 minutes on each side or until lightly golden and tender. Heat the remaining oil in a large frying pan or wok and fry the almonds, stirring constantly, until golden. Add the vegetables and stir-fry quickly until warmed through. Add the remaining soya sauce. Place the salmon steaks on 4 warmed serving plates and arrange the vegetables around each one. Serve at once.

SICHUAN-STYLE SCALLOPS

Scallops are a favourite with the Chinese. Stir-frying for 2–3 minutes is quite sufficient to cook them thoroughly while retaining their sweet flavour. They go very well with this spicy Sichuan sauce. Serve with rice and steamed vegetables.

4 teaspoons groundnut or sesame oil
1 teaspoon finely chopped fresh ginger root
2 teaspoons finely chopped spring onions
12 medium to large fresh or frozen scallops including the corals
2 teaspoons rice wine or dry sherry
2 teaspoons light soya sauce
1–2 teaspoons chilli bean sauce
2 teaspoons tomato purée
1 teaspoon sugar

Serves 4

Heat a wok or a large frying-pan. Add 3 teaspoons of the oil. Add the chopped ginger and spring onions and stir quickly for 1 minute. Next add the scallops and stir-fry them for 30 seconds. Then add the rice wine or sherry, soya sauce, chilli bean sauce, tomato purée and sugar. Continue to stir-fry for 2 minutes until the scallops are tender and thoroughly coated with the sauce. Now add the remaining oil and stir for another minute. Serve at once.

BABY SQUID IN SESAME OIL

Serve with a simple tomato salad and boiled rice or fried potatoes.

1–1½ lbs (450–675g) baby squid, cleaned and cut into rings
4 teaspoons light soya sauce
¼ teaspoon vinegar
½ teaspoon caster sugar
2 tablespoons sesame oil
Salad leaves for garnish

Serves 4

Place the squid in a bowl, pour boiling water over and leave for about 1 minute. Drain well. Mix the soya sauce, vinegar and sugar together in a small bowl. Heat the sesame oil in a frying pan and, when hot, add the squid. Toss for about 1–2 minutes; if it is cooked for too long the squid will toughen. Pour the soya mixture over the squid then transfer to a serving dish. Garnish with salad leaves and serve.

GHANAIAN BAKED TROUT WITH CHILLI SAUCE

This exotic fish dish is accompanied by a rather hot sauce, made from puréed raw vegetables and chilli pepper.

4 medium-sized trout, cleaned (head and tail removed if you wish)
Salt and freshly ground black pepper to taste
2 oz (50g) butter, melted, plus extra for greasing
1½ in (4cm) piece fresh ginger root, peeled and chopped
Juice of ½ lemon
3 red peppers, seeded and chopped
1 fresh red chilli, seeded and chopped
1 large onion, chopped
3 large tomatoes, chopped
Onion rings to garnish
Tomato slices to garnish

Serves 4

Preheat the oven to 350°F (180°C, gas mark 4). Lightly grease a large shallow baking dish with butter. Put the trout in the dish and season with salt and pepper. Pour over the melted butter and sprinkle over the ginger and lemon juice. Cover and bake in the centre of the oven for 25–30 minutes or until the fish flakes easily when pierced with a fork. Meanwhile purée the red peppers, chilli, onion, tomatoes and 1 teaspoon salt in a blender or food processor then transfer to a serving bowl. Serve the fish garnished with thinly sliced onion rings and tomatoes and accompanied with the bowl of chilli sauce.

QUICK LEMON AND GINGER CHICKEN

This is a fresh, light-tasting dish which is best served with rice or pasta and a green salad or green vegetables, such as mangetout or French beans.

1 onion, thinly sliced
1 clove garlic, crushed
1 in (2.5cm) piece fresh
  ginger root, peeled and
  grated
1 small green pepper, seeded
  and sliced
2 tablespoons sunflower oil
1 lb (450g) chicken breasts,
  skinned, boned and sliced
Juice of 1 lemon and 3 strips
  lemon peel
½ pint (275ml) chicken
  stock
1 tablespoon chopped fresh
  dill or 1 teaspoon dried
  dill
Salt and freshly ground
  black pepper to taste
2 tablespoons chopped fresh
  parsley
3 tablespoons thick yogurt
  or fromage frais

Serves 4

Gently fry the onion, garlic, ginger and green pepper in the oil for 5 minutes. Raise the heat slightly and fry the chicken for about 3 minutes until browned. Add the lemon juice and peel, the stock and the dill. Season, bring to the boil and simmer covered for 10 minutes. Stir in the parsley, then remove the pan from the heat, remove the lemon peel and mix in the yogurt or fromage frais, stirring until smooth. Reheat gently, without boiling.

MUSTARD AND TARRAGON CHICKEN CASSEROLE

4 chicken portions, skinned
2 tablespoons wholemeal
  flour
2 tablespoons sunflower oil
12 shallots
¼ pint (150ml) dry cider
½ pint (275ml) chicken
  stock
1–2 tablespoons Dijon
  mustard
1 tablespoon chopped fresh
  tarragon
Salt and freshly ground
  black pepper to taste
3 tablespoons fromage frais
  or yogurt

Serves 4

Preheat the oven to 350°F (180°C, gas mark 4). Toss the chicken portions in the flour. Heat the oil in a frying pan and brown the chicken pieces on all sides, then transfer to a shallow ovenproof dish. Fry the onions in the same oil until browned, then add the cider and cook until reduced by half. Stir in the stock, mustard, tarragon and seasoning. Bring to the boil and pour over the chicken. Cover with foil and bake in the preheated oven for about 1 hour or until the chicken is tender. Stir in the fromage frais or yogurt and serve.

PORTUGUESE CHICKEN IN PIRI-PIRI SAUCE

Chicken, onion and mushrooms are served with piri-piri sauce, a spicy mixture of chillies, lemon juice and red peppers. Serve with rice.

Juice of 1 lemon
1 small red pepper, seeded and thinly sliced, and 1 medium red pepper, seeded and coarsely sliced
2–3 fresh red chillies (or 4 if you like really hot food), seeded and chopped
4 tablespoons olive oil
Salt to taste
8 chicken drumsticks
1 onion, finely sliced
4 oz (100g) button mushrooms, cut in half
1 cinnamon stick
½ pint (275ml) water

Serves 4

Put the lemon juice, thinly sliced red pepper and red chillies in a small pan, cover and simmer gently until the pepper and chillies are softened. Purée in a blender with 1 tablespoon of the olive oil, add salt to taste then transfer to a small dish and set aside.

Heat the remaining oil in a large frying pan with a lid or in a casserole dish and add the drumsticks. Brown them on all sides and then add the onion and mushrooms. Stir over a moderate heat until the onion is softened. Add the cinnamon stick, water and 1 tablespoon of the sauce. Bring to the boil, reduce the heat, then cover and simmer until the chicken is tender, about 30 minutes. After 15 minutes add the coarsely sliced red pepper and a little more sauce if the cooking liquid is not spicy enough. Discard the cinnamon stick and serve with rice. Pass any leftover sauce separately.

CHICKEN WITH MANGO SAUCE

This is an unusual recipe from Australia, where meat and fruit are often combined in the same dish.

4 chicken breasts
3 oz (75g) butter
1 mango, peeled and stoned
1 onion, finely chopped
½ teaspoon grated lemon zest
½ chicken stock cube
1 tablespoon lemon juice
Salt and freshly ground black pepper to taste
1 stalk celery, finely chopped
2 tablespoons chopped walnuts
3 fl oz (75ml) soured cream

Serves 4

Fry the chicken breasts in two thirds of the butter over a high heat, turning them over until browned on both sides. Reduce heat and cook for 12 minutes on each side or until tender. Transfer to a serving dish, cover and keep warm. Meanwhile, purée the mango in a blender and set aside. Fry the onion gently in the remaining butter until softened but not brown. Add the mango purée, lemon zest and stock cube. Gradually stir in the lemon juice then season with salt and pepper. Cook the sauce over a high heat for 10 minutes to reduce and thicken it. Add the celery, walnuts and soured cream. Heat through gently without boiling. Coat the chicken with a little of the sauce and serve immediately, with the remaining sauce passed separately.

PENANG CHICKEN

A delightful Malaysian dish combining hot, sweet and sour tastes.

4 tablespoons vegetable oil
3 onions, finely chopped
2 cloves garlic, crushed
1–2 fresh red or green
  chillies, seeded and
  chopped
1 tablespoon soft brown
  sugar
8 chicken pieces
3 tablespoons dark soya
  sauce
3 tablespoons wine vinegar
2 tablespoons water
½ teaspoon salt

Serves 4

Heat the oil in a large saucepan or a deep frying pan. Add the onions, garlic and chillies and fry gently for 6 minutes. Stir in the sugar and continue cooking for a few more minutes. Add the chicken pieces and fry, turning frequently, until they are evenly browned. Stir in the soya sauce, vinegar, water and salt. Bring the mixture to the boil. Cover the pan, reduce the heat to low and cook for 15 minutes. Uncover the pan and continue cooking for a further 25 minutes or until the chicken is tender and cooked through.

PINE NUT AND CHICKEN PILAV

Pine nuts are quite expensive but once toasted they add a distinctive Middle Eastern flavour to a dish. This simple recipe is good for using up leftover cooked chicken. Note that cooked chicken should only be reheated if it was cooked within the previous 48 hours and then stored in the refrigerator.

2 tablespoons vegetable oil
1 lb (450g) cooked chicken, cut into bite-sized pieces
½ teaspoon ground ginger
1 teaspoon cinnamon
1 onion, finely diced
1 pint (550ml) chicken stock
8 oz (225g) long grain rice
4 oz (100g) pine nuts, dry-roasted until light brown
Salt to taste

Serves 4

Heat the oil in a heavy frying pan and brown the chicken pieces in it. Add the ginger, cinnamon and onion and sauté until the onion is softened. Remove the pan from the heat and allow to cool a little. Pour in the stock and add the rice, pine nuts and salt. Return the pan to the heat, cover and simmer for 20 minutes or until the rice is cooked and all the liquid has been absorbed. Add more stock or water if needed.

BAKED LEMON CHICKEN AND POTATOES

Once put together, this easy-to-prepare dish can be forgotten for an hour while you get on with other jobs. Serve with a lettuce and/or watercress salad.

4 chicken breasts
2 tablespoons plain flour
1 tablespoon vegetable oil
1½ lb (675g) potatoes,
  peeled and thickly sliced
Salt and freshly ground
  black pepper to taste
3 tablespoons finely chopped
  fresh parsley
3 cloves garlic, crushed
Juice of 4 lemons

Serves 4

Preheat the oven to 350°F (180°C, gas mark 4). Coat the chicken breasts with the flour. Heat the oil in a heavy frying pan and fry the chicken on both sides until lightly browned. Transfer to an ovenproof dish, arrange the potato slices around the chicken pieces, then season with salt and black pepper. Sprinkle over the parsley and garlic, pour in the lemon juice, cover and bake in the preheated oven for 1 hour or until the potatoes are cooked.

CHICKEN AND APPLE STIR-FRY

The secret of good stir-frying is to make sure you cut all the ingredients into bite-sized pieces and to stir constantly during cooking. Here is a distinctive stir-fry chicken dish. You could also try it with other ingredients such as mushrooms, water chestnuts, Chinese cabbage and so on.

3 tablespoons vegetable oil
1 lb (450g) chicken breasts, skinned and filleted and cut into strips ½ in (1.25cm) wide
1 clove garlic, crushed
1 green pepper, seeded and cut into thin strips
1 red pepper, seeded and cut into thin strips
2 oz (50g) mangetout, trimmed
Finely grated rind and juice of ½ lemon
4 oz (100g) beansprouts, washed and dried
2 tablespoons chopped fresh parsley
1 tablespoon light soya sauce
2 crisp eating apples, peeled, cored and diced

Serves 4

Heat the oil in a wok or a large frying pan. Add the chicken pieces and toss continuously over a high heat until they are sealed on all sides. Add the garlic and sauté for 2 minutes. Add the peppers and mangetout and stir-fry for a further 2 minutes. Add the remaining ingredients, cook for a further 1 or 2 minutes then serve immediately.

RICE AND CHICKEN ONE-POT

2 tablespoons vegetable oil
4 chicken breasts
6 oz (175g) long grain rice
1 pint (550ml) chicken stock
8 oz (225g) tomatoes, cut
  into quarters
1 clove garlic, crushed
7 oz (200g) can sweetcorn
  kernels, drained
Salt and freshly ground
  black pepper to taste
4 oz (100g) frozen peas

Serves 4

Heat the oil in a deep pan and fry the chicken breasts for 7–8 minutes until evenly browned on all sides. Push the chicken to one side, add the rice and fry gently for 1 minute, stirring constantly, until the rice is opaque. Stir the chicken breasts into the rice, then add the chicken stock, tomatoes, garlic, sweetcorn and salt and pepper to taste. Bring to the boil, cover and simmer gently for about 30 minutes or until the chicken and rice are tender. If the mixture becomes too dry, add a little water, or if it is too liquid, leave the lid off for a while. Add the peas, simmer to heat through, then serve.

CHICKEN IN MUSTARD SAUCE

This recipe uses only three ingredients but the finished dish is exceptionally tasty. A mild mustard such as Dijon works very well or, if you enjoy strongly flavoured food, try using prepared English mustard. Serve with boiled rice.

4 chicken breasts
4 heaped teaspoons mustard
6 fl oz (175ml) single cream

Serves 4

Preheat the oven to 375°F (190°C, gas mark 5). Prick the chicken skin then spread the top side of each chicken breast with the mustard and place them in a greased roasting tin. Bake covered in the preheated oven for about 30 minutes or until the chicken is tender. Transfer the chicken to warmed serving plates. Pour the juices and any mustard left in the tin into a small pan, stir in the cream and heat gently, stirring constantly. Pour the hot sauce over the chicken and serve.

GRILLED CHICKEN DRUMSTICKS IN FOIL

In this recipe the drumsticks are wrapped in foil with chopped courgettes and various flavourings and then cooked. In this way they retain all their flavour and moisture.

8 chicken drumsticks
2 fl oz (50ml) olive oil
8 small courgettes, chopped into slices ½ in (1.25cm) thick
4 cloves garlic, finely chopped
2 teaspoons chopped fresh basil or 1 teaspoon dried basil
Salt and freshly ground black pepper to taste
1 tablespoon tomato purée

Serves 4

Preheat the grill to medium. Brush the drumsticks with the oil and grill for about 2 minutes on each side. Cut 8 squares of foil, each one big enough to take a drumstick. Put a drumstick on each square and arrange the courgette slices around it. Sprinkle the garlic, basil and salt and black pepper over and dab a little tomato purée on top. Wrap the foil around each drumstick to form a parcel and cook the parcels under the grill for about 7 minutes on each side.

EGGS AND CHEESE

LENTIL, CHEESE AND CARROT WEDGES

Equally delicious hot or cold. Good for picnics.

8 oz (225g) red lentils
¾ pint (450ml) water
1 oz (25g) butter
1 large onion, chopped
2 carrots, grated
4 oz (100g) cheese, grated
1 teaspoon dried mixed
    herbs
1 egg
1 oz (25g) wholemeal
    breadcrumbs
Salt and freshly ground
    black pepper to taste

Serves 4

Preheat the oven to 375°F (190°C, gas mark 5). Cook the lentils in the water until the lentils are soft and all the water has been absorbed. Melt the butter in a pan and fry the onion until transparent. Add all the remaining ingredients, including the lentils, and combine thoroughly. Press into a greased 9 in (23cm) sandwich tin and bake in the preheated oven for 30 minutes. Serve either hot or cold, cut into wedges.

WATERCRESS AND GOAT'S CHEESE TART

This recipe is delicious but also quite rich. Make it now and again for a treat and serve smallish slices. A simple green salad is enough to accompany it.

12 oz (350g) shortcrust
    pastry (or make your own
    using 8 oz/225g flour)
1 oz (25g) butter
2 oz (50g) onion, finely
    chopped
1 clove garlic, crushed
1 bunch watercress
6 oz (175g) soft goat's cheese
1 teaspoon Dijon mustard
Pinch of ground nutmeg
2 eggs
¼ pint (150ml) single cream
Salt and freshly ground
    black pepper to taste

Serves 4

Preheat the oven to 400°F (200°C, gas mark 6). Roll out the pastry and use to line a 9 in (23cm) round tin. Prick the pastry base, cover with greaseproof paper, weight with dried beans or rice, and bake 'blind' for 10 minutes. Remove the paper and the dried beans or rice and continue to bake for a further 10 minutes or until the pastry is pale golden. Remove from the oven and reduce the oven temperature to 350°F (180°C, gas mark 4).

Melt the butter in a pan and sauté the onion and garlic for 3–4 minutes until golden. Add the watercress and cook for a further minute until just wilted. In a mixing bowl whisk together the watercress mixture, goat's cheese, mustard, nutmeg, eggs, cream and seasoning. Pour this filling into the flan case and bake for about 30 minutes or until puffed and golden. Serve the tart warm or cold.

EGGS IN A GREEN NEST

Eggs are cooked in a mixture of lettuce, mushrooms and garlic, then topped with cheese and nutmeg.

1 tablespoon vegetable oil
1 small Cos lettuce, finely
   shredded
4 oz (100g) mushrooms,
   sliced
2 cloves garlic, crushed
Salt and freshly ground
   black pepper to taste
4 medium or large eggs
2 oz (50g) Cheddar cheese,
   grated
A little grated nutmeg

Serves 4

Heat the oil in a large heavy frying pan or a shallow gratin dish. Add the lettuce, mushrooms and garlic and sauté, stirring, until the lettuce has wilted, about 3 minutes. Season with salt and black pepper. Make four depressions in the mixture with the back of a large spoon and break an egg into each. Cover the pan with a lid (or kitchen foil) and cook over low heat until the eggs are set, 3–5 minutes. Sprinkle cheese over each egg, grate a little nutmeg on top and serve.

PIPERADE

For a definitive Spanish flavour, serve this dish with triangles of thickly sliced bread fried in olive oil.

4 tablespoons olive oil
2 onions, thinly sliced
2 cloves garlic, thinly sliced
2 tomatoes, sliced (and skinned, if you wish)
4 peppers (mixed yellow, red or green, if you wish), seeded and coarsely chopped into rings
Salt and freshly ground black pepper to taste
6 large or medium eggs, lightly beaten

Serves 4

Heat the oil in a large heavy frying pan. Add the onions and garlic and sauté until softened but not browned. Add the tomatoes and peppers and simmer, stirring occasionally, over a low heat for 8–10 minutes. Add salt and black pepper to taste. Pour the beaten eggs into the pan and cook very slowly until they have just set. Do not turn the piperade over, just transfer it to a warmed serving dish by carefully sliding it out of the pan.

BAKED EGGS IN COURGETTES

2½ lbs (1.1 kg) courgettes,
  coarsely grated
1½ oz (40g) butter
2 tablespoons olive oil
2 cloves garlic, crushed
4 spring onions, chopped
Salt and freshly ground
  black pepper to taste
4 eggs
4 oz (100g) Cheddar cheese,
  grated

Serves 4

Preheat the oven to 350°F (180°C, gas mark 4). Sprinkle the courgettes with 1 teaspoon salt. Toss and leave for 5 minutes in a colander. Take out the courgettes by handfuls, squeezing gently to remove excess water, and spread on paper towels to drain. Courgettes prepared this way do not become soggy when cooked.

Heat the butter and oil together in a large frying pan, add the garlic and spring onions and cook until softened. Add the courgettes, stirring constantly. Cook uncovered for 8 minutes on a low heat, stirring occasionally, then season to taste. Put the courgette mixture in a greased shallow dish, make 4 hollows in the mixture and break an egg into each hollow. Sprinkle each egg with the grated cheese then bake in the preheated oven for about 15 minutes. The yolks should still be a little soft.

EGGAH WITH NOODLES AND CHICKEN

Eggah is an Arabian omelette. It should be firm and thick, rather like an egg cake. Eggah is good hot or cold and it also makes an excellent picnic dish.

2 pints (1.1 litres) chicken
    stock or water
4 oz (100g) egg noodles
6 eggs
1 teaspoon salt
½ teaspoon black pepper
Pinch of cayenne pepper
2 teaspoons paprika
1 teaspoon ground cumin
1 clove garlic, crushed
8 oz (225g) cooked chicken,
    diced
2 oz (50g) butter

Serves 4–6

Bring the chicken stock or water to the boil in a large saucepan. Add the noodles, cover and simmer for 6 minutes, or until the noodles are tender. Drain and set aside. Beat the eggs, salt, black pepper, cayenne pepper, paprika, cumin and garlic together with a wire whisk until the mixture is light and frothy. Stir in the cooked chicken and the noodles. Melt the butter in a large frying pan over moderate heat. Reduce the heat to low and pour in the chicken and egg mixture. Cook slowly for 20–30 minutes, or until the underside is golden brown and the egg is cooked. Preheat the grill to high. Place the pan under the grill for 5 minutes, or until the top of the eggah is golden brown. Serve cut into wedges.

POACHED EGG AND BROCCOLI GRATIN

A simple but tasty lunch dish, reputed to be a favourite of Zwingli, the famous German theologian.

1½ lb (675g) broccoli, chopped
1 oz (25g) butter
1 teaspoon salt
½ teaspoon black pepper
1 teaspoon lemon jucie
4 eggs
2 oz (50g) dried wholemeal breadcrumbs
2 oz (50g) Parmesan cheese, freshly grated

Serves 4

Cook the broccoli in boiling salted water until tender, 8–10 minutes. Drain and purée in a blender or food processor. Pour into a heatproof serving dish, dot over half the butter and sprinkle over the salt, pepper and lemon juice. Poach the eggs, then arrange them on the broccoli purée and cover with the breadcrumbs and cheese. Dot over the remaining butter. Cook under a hot grill for 5 minutes until golden brown.

OMELETTE ARNOLD BENNETT

One of the best omelettes ever! A classic dish, originally created for the writer Arnold Bennett by the Savoy Grill in London.

2 oz (50g) butter
¼ pint (150ml) whipping cream
6 oz (175g) smoked haddock, cooked and flaked
6 eggs, separated
Salt and freshly ground black pepper to taste
2 oz (50g) Parmesan cheese, freshly grated

Serves 4

Melt half the butter in a pan, add 2 tablespoons of the cream and all the flaked haddock and toss over high heat for 2–3 minutes. Leave to cool. Beat the egg yolks with 1 tablespoon of the remaining cream and season to taste. Whip the egg whites lightly until soft peaks form, then fold them into the yolks with the haddock mixture and half the cheese. Melt the remaining butter in a large frying pan and cook the omelette. Do not fold, but slide on to a large, warmed dish. Sprinkle on the rest of the cheese and pour the remaining cream over it. Brown quickly under a hot grill and serve immediately.

SHERRY EGGS AND TOMATOES

A quick and convenient lunch dish. Serve with crusty French bread and a green leaf salad.

6 eggs
1½ tablespoons medium
  sherry
Pinch of salt
2 tablespoons vegetable oil
1¼ lbs (550g) tomatoes,
  skinned and thickly sliced
4 tablespoons vegetable
  stock
2 spring onions, finely
  chopped

Serves 4

Beat the eggs with the sherry and salt. Heat the oil in a frying pan and fry the tomato slices over a moderate heat. Add a little salt and then the beaten egg mixture. Cook, stirring, for 1 minute, as for scrambled eggs. Pour in the stock and cook for a further minute. Serve immediately, very hot, sprinkled with the chopped spring onions.

SPINACH ROLLED OMELETTE

This is a Westernized version of the Japanese rolled omelette. It makes an unusual and appetizing starter, or can be served as a main course with a salad and/or vegetables.

4 eggs
1 teaspoon soya sauce
¼ teaspoon ground ginger
1 teaspoon sugar
1 tablespoon plain flour, finely sifted
1 tablespoon vegetable oil
10 young spinach leaves, washed and drained
1 stalk celery, cut into long, thin strips

Serves 2 as a main course, 4 as a starter

Beat together the eggs, soya sauce, ginger, sugar and flour to form a smooth batter. Heat a heavy 9 in (23cm) frying pan over a moderate heat until hot, then lightly brush it with the oil. Pour in half the batter and tilt the pan so that the mixture spreads evenly. Cook until the underside is just soft but not browned. Turn the omelette over and cook the other side. Transfer the omelette to a plate and, if you wish, keep warm in a preheated moderate oven. Make a second omelette with the remaining batter. Trim each omelette into an approximate rectangle and keep the trimmings. Place one omelette on top of the other on a bamboo mat or slightly damp cloth and layer the omelette trimmings, the spinach leaves and the celery strips across one end. Roll the omelette up like a Swiss roll, then remove the bamboo mat or cloth. Slice the roll into 1 in (2.5cm) thick pieces and serve.

SPINACH TORTILLA

Tortilla, the Spanish potato omelette, is a favourite at the tapas counter. Here it is served hot but it's just as good cold. Perfect for a packed lunch or picnic.

1 lb (450g) frozen spinach, thawed
8 oz (225g) Edam cheese, grated
6 oz (150g) potatoes, finely diced
1 carrot, grated
4 oz (100g) onion, finely chopped
1 clove garlic, crushed
4 eggs
A little milk
Salt and freshly ground black pepper to taste

Serves 4

Preheat the oven to 375°F (190°C, gas mark 5). Drain and roughly chop the spinach. Mix together half the cheese, the potatoes, carrot, onion, garlic and spinach. Beat the eggs with a little milk, season, and stir into the vegetable mixture. Pour into a large greased baking dish and sprinkle the remaining cheese over the top. Bake in the preheated oven for 30 minutes until set and golden brown. Serve hot with good, crusty bread and a tomato salad.

EGG BAMBOO

An unusual but easy egg dish from the Chinese kitchen.

4 eggs
¼ teaspoon salt
¼ teaspoon freshly ground
 black pepper
2 teaspoons rice vinegar or
 cider vinegar
2 tablespoons cooking oil
4 oz (100g) canned bamboo
 shoots, cut into thin strips
1 teaspoon soya sauce
½ teaspoon sugar
1 teaspoon sesame oil or
 other vegetable oil
1 spring onion, finely
 chopped

**Serves 2–4 (starter/main
course)**

Beat the eggs in a bowl and mix in the salt, pepper and vinegar. Heat 1 tablespoon of the oil in a wok or large frying pan and stir-fry the bamboo shoots for 1 minute. Sprinkle with the soya sauce and sugar and fry for a further 30 seconds. Remove the bamboo shoots and any liquid from the pan. Heat the remaining oil in the pan and pour in the egg mixture. Return the bamboo shoots and their liquid to the pan and stir together until the egg begins to set. Stir in the sesame oil and serve garnished with the chopped spring onion.

LEEK, APPLE AND MOZZARELLA TART

Leek, apple and mozzarella cheese have a great affinity with each other, and as a tart filling the combination is one league ahead of its more common cousin, cheese and onion.

2 lb (900g) leeks, washed and chopped into 1 in (2.5cm) lengths
2 oz (50g) butter
4 tablespoons chopped fresh parsley
12 oz (350g) puff pastry
2 large Bramley apples, peeled, cored and sliced
12 oz (350g) mozzarella cheese, sliced
Salt and freshly ground black pepper to taste
1 egg, beaten

Serves 4–6

Preheat the oven to 400°F (200°C, gas mark 6). Fry the leeks gently in the butter with the parsley for a few minutes until the leeks are softened but still crunchy. Remove from the heat and set aside. Roll out half the pastry and use to line a baking tray approximately 11 in × 7 in (27.5cm × 17.5cm). Spread the leeks over the pastry, then cover with the apple slices and arrange the mozzarella slices on top. Season lightly. Roll out the remaining pastry until it is slightly bigger than the tin and place on top of the filling. Trim and seal the edges, then roll the edges over to form a crust. Brush with the beaten egg and bake in the top of the preheated oven until golden brown, about 25 minutes.

SPANAKOPITTA

3 eggs
1 lb (450g) frozen spinach, thawed, drained and roughly chopped
4 oz (100g) feta cheese, crumbled
Salt and freshly ground black pepper to taste
8 oz (225g) filo pastry
3 oz (75g) butter, melted, plus extra for greasing

Serves 4

Preheat the oven to 375°F (190°C, gas mark 5). Beat the eggs in a large bowl then stir in the chopped spinach and the crumbled feta. Season with lots of black pepper and a little salt. Butter a deep, oblong pie dish and put the filling in it. Unroll the filo pastry onto a flat surface and cover with a damp tea towel. Take the top sheet, brush with melted butter and lay it on top of the spinach mixture. Tuck in the ends. Continue to paint each sheet of filo with butter and layer them on top of each other until all the pastry is used up. Cut through the layers in a diamond pattern with a sharp knife. Brush the top with the last of the butter and bake until golden brown and crisp, about 35 minutes. Serve hot or lukewarm, cut into squares.

CREOLE BANANAS

A rum-flavoured treat from Louisiana.

4 large, ripe bananas, peeled
  and cut lengthwise in half
1½ oz (40g) butter
2 oz (50g) Demerara sugar
3 fl oz (75ml) dark rum
Juice of 1 lemon or lime
A little grated nutmeg

Serves 4

Preheat the oven to 350°F (180°C, gas mark 4). Arrange the bananas in a single layer in a shallow baking dish. Dot with the butter, sprinkle with the sugar and pour over the rum and lemon or lime juice. Dust with a few pinches of nutmeg. Bake in the preheated oven for 30–35 minutes or until the sauce is very thick. Serve hot or cold.

EXOTIC FRUIT SALAD

Papayas are the main ingredient in this recipe. Good specimens should have smooth, green to yellow skin and pink, sweet flesh.

2 ripe but firm papayas,
  peeled, quartered and
  seeded
½ small pineapple, peeled,
  cored and finely chopped
4 oz (100g) fresh dates,
  stoned and thinly sliced
2 oz (50g) shredded coconut,
  gently toasted in a dry pan
2 limes, cut into wedges

Serves 4

Place the papaya quarters on 4 small white serving plates. Combine the pineapple and dates and spoon the mixture over the papaya quarters. Garnish with the toasted coconut and serve with the lime wedges.

RASPBERRY YOGURT FOOL

*The simplest of desserts but delicious and made in an instant.
Handy to use when a punnet of raspberries is just past its best for
eating fresh.*

8 oz (225g) raspberries
2 teaspoons runny honey
1¼ pints (700ml) plain
  yogurt

Serves 4

Set aside 4 raspberries then mash the remaining berries gently with a fork and stir them into the yogurt with the honey. Divide between 4 glasses, decorate each with a reserved raspberry and serve.

BLACKBERRY FRUIT LAYER

6 oz (175g) medium-fat curd cheese
10 oz (275g) thick-set plain yogurt
14 oz (400g) can blackberries in natural juice, or fresh blackberries (see below)
1 tablespoon sherry
1 oz (25g) hazelnuts, chopped (optional)

TO USE FRESH BLACKBERRIES:
12 oz (350g) fresh blackberries, washed and drained
1–2 oz (25–30g) castor sugar

Serves 4

Put the blackberries in a pan with the sugar and simmer gently for 5 minutes. Allow to cool.

Put the curd cheese in a bowl and whisk in the yogurt. Set aside a few blackberries for decoration and mix the rest, with their juice, with the sherry. Spoon half of the yogurt and cheese mixture into 4 tall glasses. Spoon over the blackberries and sherry, then cover with the remaining yogurt and cheese mixture. Decorate each glass with the reserved blackberries and the chopped hazelnuts, if using. Serve chilled.

RASPBERRY SORBET

Very fast to prepare (after a tiny amount of advance planning) and delicious.

1 lb (450g) frozen
   raspberries
2 bananas, peeled, cut into
   slices ½ in (1.25cm) thick,
   then frozen

Serves 4

Remove the fruit from the freezer. Leave at room temperature for 5 minutes then purée together in a blender or food processor. Pour into glasses and serve. In season you could garnish each portion with 2 or 3 fresh raspberries.

PINEAPPLE AND NUT CRUNCH

3 oz (75g) butter
4 oz (100g) wheatmeal
  biscuits, crushed
1 oz (25g) soft brown sugar
2 oz (50g) nuts of your
  choice, chopped
12 oz (350g) canned
  pineapple chunks, drained

Serves 4

Melt the butter in a saucepan, add the biscuit crumbs, and cook for 2 minutes or until golden brown and crisp, stirring constantly. Cool, then stir in the sugar and chopped nuts. Set aside 4 pieces of pineapple. Divide half the remaining pineapple between 4 glasses then cover with half the crunchy mixture. Repeat the layers. Top with the reserved pineapple pieces and serve chilled, accompanied by plain yogurt if you wish.

PEACHES WITH RASPBERRY SAUCE

This recipe was inspired by the French chef Georges Blanc.

8 oz (225g) fresh raspberries
3 oz (75g) icing sugar
Juice of 1 lemon
4 large, ripe peaches, peeled,
  stoned and thinly sliced
8 fresh basil sprigs for
  garnish

Serves 4

Purée the raspberries with the icing sugar in a blender, then strain through a sieve to remove the pips, using the back of a wooden spoon to press the purée through. Stir half the lemon juice into the raspberry purée, then refrigerate until chilled.

Brush the peach slices with the remaining lemon juice and chill them in the refrigerator. Pour the sauce onto 4 small plates, arrange the peach slices on top and garnish with the basil sprigs. Serve immediately.

RHUBARB FOOL

Only a fool could fail to enjoy this very English dish.

1 lb (450g) rhubarb, washed, trimmed and sliced
4 oz (100g) soft brown sugar
1 teaspoon allspice
¼ pint (150ml) whipping cream
¼ pint (150ml) low-fat yogurt

Serves 4

Put the rhubarb and sugar into a saucepan with the allspice. Cook over a low heat until tender, then leave to cool. Meanwhile, whip the cream until stiff, then stir in the yogurt. When the rhubarb is cool fold in the cream and yogurt mixture. Pour into tall glasses and serve chilled, with crisp, little biscuits.

CHOCOLATE PEARS

1 tablespoon custard powder
1 teaspoon instant coffee
1 teaspoon cocoa powder
½ pint (275ml) milk
1 oz (25g) soft brown sugar
½ teaspoon vanilla essence
4 oz (100g) fromage frais
14 oz (400g) tinned, drained pear halves, or fresh pears (see below)
Chopped walnuts and grated nutmeg for garnish

TO USE FRESH PEARS:
4 firm dessert pears, peeled, cored and cut in half lengthwise
2 oz (50g) granulated sugar
8 fl oz (225ml) water

Serves 4

Put the sugar and water in a small saucepan, just big enough to hold the pear halves. Bring to the boil and boil for 3 minutes. Add the pear halves and simmer covered until tender, about 15 minutes (time depends on ripeness and size). Allow to cool.

Blend the custard, coffee and cocoa powders with a little of the milk. Heat the rest of the milk in a pan until nearly boiling then stir in the sugar. Pour in the powdered mixture and stir constantly until the custard thickens. Remove from the heat, leave to cool slightly then stir in the vanilla essence.

Put the fromage frais in a bowl and beat with a wooden spoon to soften. Gradually work in the custard, whisking with a wire whisk if necessary, until smooth. Put the pear halves, flat side down in individual dishes. Spoon the chocolate sauce over them and sprinkle with chopped walnuts and grated nutmeg. Serve lukewarm or cold.

BANANA SPLITS

Simply delicious! Lovely for breakfast too . . .

4 small, ripe bananas
¼ pint (150ml) Greek yogurt
8 oz (225g) strawberries
1 oz (25g) icing sugar

Serves 4

Peel the bananas and cut them lengthwise in half. Sandwich the banana halves together with the Greek yogurt. Purée the strawberries in a blender with the icing sugar then strain through a nylon sieve. Pour this sauce over the bananas and serve.

Note You can use any fruit for the sauce – raspberries, blackberries, apricots etc. They can be fresh or canned.

Exotic Fruits

Grown in lands that are hot and sunny during our winter time, the cheerful colours and different flavours and textures of imported exotic fruits can brighten up and add a touch of glamour to an ordinary dish, or provide a simple but unusual dessert on their own. They can also contribute to our daily needs for fresh vitamins and minerals, especially useful in warding off seasonal colds.

Improved transportation means that nowadays we can enjoy these exotic fruits within days of their being picked thousands of miles away. Good supplies and their increased popularity have also brought prices down. The varieties I have chosen to describe here are those most commonly available in the shops. Some, like dates and figs, are well known as dried fruits, but the fresh varieties are very different and worth discovering. Buy only good specimens of any exotic fruit since the bruised ones will go off quickly. Handle them carefully and use as soon as they are fully ripe. Remember that a small amount of exotic fruit, such as a chopped mango, a few sliced figs or a couple of lychees, are all you need to liven up a fruit or vegetable salad.

Dates

Fresh dates are imported all year around, mainly from Israel, but the best varieties are available from October to February. They should be moist and plump with a dark brown shiny skin. They can be eaten raw, and are also good stuffed with savoury or sweet fillings such as soft cheese or marzipan. In the Middle East they are often served with cardamom-flavoured yogurt.

Figs

The fig is one of the most ancient of cultivated fruits and because of its succulent flavour and soft and juicy seed-filled flesh it has a carnal reputation. Fresh figs are very tender and need to be handled carefully. There are many varieties and the outer skin may be white, green, purple or black. The skin should peel easily off ripe specimens but it is edible and can be left on. Figs are good on their own or with smoked cheese as a starter, or with yogurt or cream as a dessert, or sliced in fruit salads.

Kumquats

Kumquats are related to the citrus family and they look like tiny, slightly elongated oranges. *Kum kwot* is, in fact, Cantonese for golden orange. However, their skin is edible and the fruit is eaten whole. At their best they are firm with a rich, aromatic smell and sweet-sour taste. Good on their own as a simple dessert with coffee, or cooked gently in a little water and served as a garnish to poultry dishes.

Lychees

Tinned lychees are an ubiquitous dessert in Chinese restaurants but the fresh variety, which has a more fragrant smell and flavoursome taste, is much more interesting. They have a thin, reddish-brown shell, rough and scaly in texture. It peels off easily to reveal the white, translucent flesh of the fruit. This surrounds a single shiny brown seed which is too bitter to eat. Choose lychees with full and firm shells and store them in a refrigerator. Excellent on their own or in fruit salads or served with cream, ice-cream or sorbet.

Mango

There are literally hundreds of varieties of mango and in areas where they grow, such as South-East Asia and the West Indies, they are as varied, popular and common as apples in the West. All unripe mangoes are dark green but they can ripen to yellow, red, orange, pink or purple. The flesh, however, is nearly always pale orange. It is sweet and very juicy. Stoning a mango without covering oneself in juice is an art, but one worth learning. First of all, cut a thick slice lengthwise down each side of the flat central stone, as close to the stone as possible. This leaves a thin central slice in which the stone is embedded. Scoop the flesh from the two halves with a spoon and cut around the stone in the central slice to remove as much flesh as possible. Eat mango on its own or in fruit salads, or made into ice cream or sorbet, or added to a cheesecake filling for flavour and colour. In Thailand, sliced mango is traditionally served with sweet, sticky rice. Mangoes are rich in vitamins, especially vitamin A.

Papaya (Paw Paw)

This pear-shaped fruit with a smooth skin is available all year round. It is green when unripe, turning to a deep yellow colour when ripe. The taste resembles a cross between peaches and melons, and is slightly scented and sweet. To eat papaya, cut in half lengthwise, scoop out the seeds and serve with a sprinkling of lime or lemon juice. Alternatively serve lightly salted and stuffed with cottage cheese. Diced or sliced, papayas are perfect in tropical fruit salads or as a base for mousses, fools and ice-creams.

Passion Fruit

A small, purple egg-shaped fruit. When ripe the hard leathery skin becomes wrinkled. Passion fruit are perfect for eating on their own. Simply cut in half and scoop out the sweet juicy seeds with a spoon. Or heat the scooped-out flesh in a pan, dilute with a little apple juice and serve with grilled fish – it's especially good with salmon.

Persimmon (Sharon Fruit)

A bright orange, tomato-like fruit originally from Japan. It is suitable for eating only when fully ripe, when the flesh is sweet, soft and pulpy. Unripe, persimmons are sour and astringent. Sharon fruit is an 'improved' persimmon developed by the Israelis. It can be eaten while still firm and the skin and seeds are also edible. To eat persimmons, slice off the top and scoop out the pulp. Sharon fruit can be sliced and added to salads or fruit salads. They are also good combined with slices of avocado in a vinaigrette dressing.

Pomegranate

A familiar exotic fruit, but nevertheless worth including here for its variety of uses. Cut in half and scoop out the seeds for use in salads or in fruit cocktails. The juice (make sure not to crush the seeds when squeezing the fruit or the juice will be too bitter) is good for flavouring jellies, sorbets and ice-cream, or in sauces for poultry and fish dishes. Grenadine syrup is made from pomegranate juice. Eaten raw, the seeds and surrounding flesh produce a delicious sweet-sour taste.

Star Fruit (Carambola)

Pale, shiny yellow-green waxy skin surrounds this odd but attractive five-sided fruit. The translucent flesh is crisp and juicy with an aromatic, mildly acidic flavour. The whole fruit is edible. Simply slice crosswise to produce star-shaped sections. Serve in salads, with cheese or nuts or as a garnish to poultry.

CONVERSION TABLES

Weights and Measures

Imperial / metric

Weights	
Imperial	*Approximate metric equivalent*
½ oz	15g
1 oz	25g
2 oz	50g
3 oz	75g
4 oz	100g
5 oz	150g
6 oz	175g
7 oz	200g
8 oz	225g
9 oz	250g
10 oz	275g
11 oz	300g
12 oz	350g
13 oz	375g
14 oz	400g
15 oz	425g
1 lb	450g
2 lb	900g
3 lb	1.4 kg

Exact conversion: 1 oz = 28.35g

Imperial / metric

Liquids

Imperial	Approximate metric equivalent
¼ teaspoon	1.25ml
½ teaspoon	2.5ml
1 teaspoon	5ml
2 teaspoons	10ml
1 tablespoon	15ml
2 tablespoons	30ml
3 tablespoons	45ml
1 fl oz	25ml
2 fl oz	50ml
3 fl oz	75ml
4 fl oz	100ml
5 fl oz (¼ pint)	150ml
6 fl oz	175ml
7 fl oz	200ml
8 fl oz	225ml
9 fl oz	250ml
10 fl oz (½ pint)	275ml
15 fl oz (¾ pint)	450ml
20 fl oz (1 pint)	550ml
1¾ pints	1 litre
2 pints	1.1 litres

Oven temperatures

°F	°C	Gas mark
225	110	¼
250	130	½
275	140	1
300	150	2
325	170	3
350	180	4
375	190	5
400	200	6
425	220	7
450	230	8
475	240	9

British and American equivalents

This book was written for a British readership. To help the American cook with the system of measurement used, here is a conversion table showing imperial weights with their American cup equivalent.

British	*American*
8 fl oz	1 cup
½ pint/10 fl oz	1¼ cups
16 fl oz	1 pint
1 pint/20 fl oz	2½ cups
2 pints/40 fl oz	2½ pints = 5 cups
2 tablespoons	⅛ cup/1½ tablespoons
8 tablespoons	½ cup
4 oz ground almonds	1 cup
5 oz almonds, unblanched	1 cup
4½ oz dried apricots	1 cup
7 oz aubergines, diced	1 cup
6 oz bamboo shoots, drained and sliced	1 cup
4 oz beancurd, drained	1 cup
6 oz beans (canned)	1 cup
3 oz beansprouts	1 cup
3½ oz broccoli (fresh), sliced	1 cup
4 oz bulgar wheat	1 cup
4 oz butter	1 stick
8 oz butter	1 cup
4 oz cabbage, shredded, firmly packed	1 cup
4 oz cauliflower, in florets	1 cup
4 oz cheese, grated	1 cup
4 oz cooked chickpeas	1 cup
2 oz flaked, unsweetened coconut	1 cup
3½ oz coriander seeds	1 cup
4 oz sweetcorn kernels	1 cup
6 oz cornflour	1 cup
5 oz courgettes, sliced	1 cup
3½ oz cumin seeds	1 cup
8 oz cooking dates	1 cup

British	American
4½ oz wholewheat flour	1 cup
4 oz white flour	1 cup
4 oz green beans, chopped	1 cup
7 oz dried lentils	1 cup
7 oz cooked lentils	1 cup
3½ oz mangetout	1 cup
9 oz miso (Japanese soya bean paste)	1 cup
2 oz broken noodles	1 cup
6 oz diced onion	1 cup
2 oz parsley, finely chopped	1 cup
6 oz peanut butter	1 cup
5 oz peanuts	1 cup
3½ oz black peppercorns	1 cup
6 oz canned pineapple chunks, drained	1 cup
6 oz raisins *or* sultanas	1 cup
8 oz dry rice (brown or white)	1¼ cups
6 oz sesame seeds	1 cup
8 oz cooked spinach	1¼ cups
1 lb raw spinach	5 cups
6½ oz cooked red beans	1 cup
8 oz granulated sugar	1 cup
6 oz brown sugar	1 cup
9 oz canned tomatoes	1 cup
8 oz tomatoes	2 medium tomatoes
9 oz tomato purée	1 cup
7 oz vegetable fat	1 cup
4 oz walnuts, chopped	1 cup
6½ oz water chestnuts, drained	1 cup
1 oz yeast	½ cup

INDEX